NEW DIRECTIONS FOR INSTITUTIONAL RESEARCH

J. Fredericks Volkwein, *State University of New York at Albany*
EDITOR-IN-CHIEF

Larry H. Litten, *Consortium on Financing Higher Education,*
Cambridge, Massachusetts
ASSOCIATE EDITOR

Forecasting and Managing Enrollment and Revenue: An Overview of Current Trends, Issues, and Methods

Daniel T. Layzell
MGT of America, Inc.

EDITOR

Number 93, Spring 1997

JOSSEY-BASS PUBLISHERS
San Francisco

FORECASTING AND MANAGING ENROLLMENT AND REVENUE:
AN OVERVIEW OF CURRENT TRENDS, ISSUES, AND METHODS
Daniel T. Layzell (ed.)
New Directions for Institutional Research, no. 93
Volume XXIV, Number 1
J. Fredericks Volkwein, Editor-in-Chief

New Directions for Institutional Research is indexed in *College Student
Personnel Abstracts, Contents Pages in Education,* and *Current Index to Jour-
nals in Education* (ERIC).

Microfilm copies of issues and articles are available in 16mm and 35mm,
as well as microfiche in 105mm, through University Microfilms Inc., 300
North Zeeb Road, Ann Arbor, Michigan 48106-1346.

ISSN 0271-0579   ISBN 0-7879-9850-8

NEW DIRECTIONS FOR INSTITUTIONAL RESEARCH is part of The Jossey-Bass
Higher and Adult Education Series and is published quarterly by Jossey-
Bass Inc., Publishers, 350 Sansome Street, San Francisco, California
94104-1342 (publication number USPS 098-830). Periodicals postage
paid at San Francisco, California, and at additional mailing offices. POST-
MASTER: Send address changes to New Directions for Institutional Re-
search, Jossey-Bass Inc., Publishers, 350 Sansome Street, San Francisco,
California 94104-1342.

SUBSCRIPTIONS cost $52.00 for individuals and $79.00 for institutions,
agencies, and libraries.

EDITORIAL CORRESPONDENCE should be sent to J. Fredericks Volkwein,
Institutional Research, Administration 241, State University of New York
at Albany, Albany, NY 12222.

Photograph of the library by Michael Graves at San Juan Capistrano by
Chad Slattery © 1984. All rights reserved.

 Manufactured in the United States of America on Lyons Falls Turin
Book. This paper is acid-free and 100 percent totally chlorine-free.

THE ASSOCIATION FOR INSTITUTIONAL RESEARCH was created in 1966 to benefit, assist, and advance research leading to improved understanding, planning, and operation of institutions of higher education. Publication policy is set by its Publications Board.

For information about the Association for Institutional Research, write to the following address:

AIR Executive Office
114 Stone Building
Florida State University
Tallahassee, FL 32306-3038

(904) 644-4470

air@mailer.fsu.edu
www.fsu.edu/~air/home.htm

CONTENTS

EDITOR'S NOTES

Once upon a time, or so the story goes, colleges and universities were able to operate from year to year without worrying too much about the details of the future. Revenues were ample, if not abundant, for meeting the academic, physical, and personnel needs of the institution. Enrollments were adequate to maintain core offerings and, in many instances, to develop new programs for the institution. In the halls of state legislatures, public colleges and universities and their leaders were held in high esteem for the good works they did for the students, citizens, and economic life of the state. Higher education was clearly a growth industry.

Whether or not this tale was true at the time, the picture for institutions of higher education is now completely different. State and federal funding for higher education is becoming increasingly scarce due to competition from other areas of government and to a general sense of public discontent with government and its institutions. In many states, several consecutive years of stagnant budgets or budget cuts have stretched campus finances and impaired the services provided. Because of this, colleges and universities are beginning to rely more on student tuition revenues to fund operational costs. But given the high level of public concern with the rising cost of a college education, this practice has limits.

On the enrollment side of this picture, there is feast and famine. Some states (for example, the western states) and some sectors of higher education are faced with record levels of students applying for admission. On the other hand, other areas of higher education are struggling to maintain the students they have, some with little luck.

These new realities of higher education indicate a need for a more sophisticated approach to dealing with the demographic and economic uncertainties faced by institutions of higher education. No longer will laissez-faire approaches to planning be adequate. Thus, the purpose of this *New Directions for Institutional Research* volume is to provide an overview of the contextual, practical, and technical aspects of enrollment and revenue forecasting and management. The major topics covered in this volume include the demographic, economic, and financial trends affecting enrollment and revenue management and forecasting in higher education; practical examples and issues pertaining to enrollment and to revenue management and forecasting (for both public and private institutions); current methods and techniques of enrollment and revenue forecasting in higher education; and an evaluation of lessons learned in these areas.

As resources become scarcer in colleges and universities, institutional research professionals are increasingly called upon to help divine trends and likely scenarios in enrollment demand at various levels of aggregation and to provide analytical support to budget-finance offices in revenue estimation. Thus, this volume will be of direct interest to institutional researchers. Also, as institutions of higher education develop more cross-functional approaches to their activities and to problem solving, professionals outside the field of institutional research are increasingly being called upon to serve on enrollment management committees. Further, senior administrators are finding it necessary to become conversant in both enrollment and revenue estimation and in forecasting issues in their interactions with governing board members and external constituencies (for example, state coordinating boards.)

Chapter One, by Robin Etter Zúñiga, outlines the major demographic trends affecting higher education enrollments over the past several years, with an assessment of prospects for the future.

Chapter Two, by Arthur Hauptman, discusses the economic and financial trends influencing higher education enrollments and revenues, both now and in the future.

Chapter Three, by Nathan Peters and Sue Keihn, provides a historical overview of the enrollment management policies of the University of Wisconsin System since 1987, including the events leading up to these policies, the impact to date, and the plans for the future in the face of significant budget reductions.

Chapter Four, by James Day, focuses specifically on the unique issues faced by private institutions in planning enrollments and anticipating revenues.

Chapter Five, by Paul Brinkman and Chuck McIntyre, discusses the practical and technical aspects of forecasting enrollments, primarily from an institutional level.

Chapter Six, by Kent Caruthers and Cathi Wentworth, focuses on the practical and technical aspects of forecasting institutional revenues from all sources.

Chapter Seven, which I wrote, synthesizes the major points of the chapter authors and provides some implications for the practice of institutional research. It also offers some additional resources for the interested reader.

I would like to thank all of the authors for their contributions to this volume and their cooperation during this project. The high quality of their chapters and the equally high levels of professionalism made my job as editor a true pleasure.

Daniel T. Layzell
Editor

DANIEL T. LAYZELL is senior associate with MGT of America, Inc., a higher education consulting firm in Tallahassee, Florida. He was previously (until March 1997) director of policy analysis and research for the University of Wisconsin System.

A dramatic increase in the pool of college-age students in the next twenty years is inevitable, but will this necessarily lead to dramatic increases in higher education enrollments?

Demographic Trends and Projections Affecting Higher Education

Robin Etter Zúñiga

Prior to World War II, higher education was both highly selective and quite exclusive. Attendance was generally limited to those with proven intellectual ability and the economic means to pay their own way. In this environment, institutions had no need for enrollment projections. The adoption of the GI bill and the emergence of federal financial aid programs, however, changed the higher education landscape. Starting in the 1950s, higher education enrollments grew steadily. The number of public higher education institutions increased, and most higher education leaders and policymakers began to perceive access as one of the most important missions of public institutions. Demographics took on a new importance as planners tried to find ways to accommodate increasing enrollment demand as the postwar baby boom came of age and later to maintain stable enrollments when the college-age population declined.

In the 1990s, higher education faces a new dilemma. The children of the postwar–baby boom generation began reaching college-going age in the mid 1990s. Based on demographic trends, higher education planners project significant increases in enrollment demand as we enter the twenty-first century. Will higher education be able to accommodate this demand?

This chapter discusses the demographic trends that are leading higher education planners to project significant increases in enrollments between now and the first part of the twenty-first century. It examines the impact that the *baby boom–echo* or *tidal wave II*[1] generation and the changes in the over twenty-four-year-old population will have on enrollments and discusses why actual higher education enrollments may fall short of these projections.

Baby Boom–Echo Generation Comes of Age

The postwar baby boom placed a heavy burden on educational resources in the 1960s and early 1970s. From 1955 through 1964, more than four million babies were born in the United States each year (Ventura and others, 1996, p. 28). As these children matured, undergraduate enrollments increased dramatically, around 45 percent between 1969 and 1979 when the postwar–baby boom generation reached its peak (U.S. Department of Education, 1995a, p. 176).

As the youngest of the postwar–baby boom generation matured, the size of the traditional college-age population stabilized. The number of births per year declined through the mid 1970s, resulting in a smaller pool of college-age students in the early 1990s (Ventura and others, 1996). The high school graduating class of 1993 was 26 percent smaller than the class of 1979 (U.S. Department of Education, 1995a, p. 108).

However, the anticipated declines in higher education enrollments, resulting from the decline in the college-age population, never materialized. Undergraduate enrollments continued to grow in the 1980s, by more than 22 percent between 1980 and 1993 (U.S. Department of Education, 1995b, p. 26). This growth resulted from increased participation rates among recent high school graduates and from the impact of the postwar–baby boom generation on enrollments of students over age twenty-four. College participation rates have increased steadily since the early 1980s. Almost 62 percent of recent high school graduates were enrolled in college in 1994, compared to only 49 percent in 1980 (U.S. Department of Education, 1995a, p. 188). Moreover, as the postwar–baby boom generation matured, the number of persons over age twenty-four who were enrolled in undergraduate programs rose from 38 percent to 44 percent of total enrollments, an increase of 38 percent between 1980 and 1993 (U.S. Department of Education, 1995a, p. 178).

As we enter the twenty-first century, new demographic pressures are mounting. The two primary factors driving population increases in the United States, international immigration and natural increase (the number of births over deaths), both increased during the 1980s.

Between 1981 and 1990, more immigrants arrived in the United States than during any ten-year period since 1910[2]. International immigration in fiscal year 1993 accounted for nearly one-third (32 percent) of the total United States population increase (natural increase plus net immigration)[3]. Border and coastal states such as California, New York, Florida, Texas, and New Jersey have had the largest influx of international immigrants. Almost 70 percent of all international immigrants in 1992 intended to reside in one of these five states (U.S. Immigration and Naturalization Service, 1996). In California, New York, and New Jersey, net international immigration helped compensate for significant net domestic out-migration in the early 1990s (U.S. Bureau of the Census, 1996a).

Immigration influences demand for education in two ways. The first way is the direct impact the immigration of school- and college-age children has on enrollments. In 1994, 6.5 percent of the United States' school- and college-age population (five to twenty-four years of age) were foreign-born. In popular destinations like California (21 percent), Florida (11 percent), and New York (10 percent), the foreign-born make up a more significant portion of the school- and college-age population (U.S. Bureau of the Census, 1994a; 1996c). The U.S. Bureau of the Census (1996b) projects that approximately 7,724 children between the ages of five and eighteen will immigrate to the United States per year over the next thirty years—adding approximately .01 percent annually to the school-age population. The second way is the impact the immigration of women of childbearing age (defined as fifteen to forty-four years of age) has on the rate of natural increase. Foreign-born women made up approximately 11 percent of all women of childbearing age in the United States in 1994 (U.S. Bureau of the Census, 1994a; 1996c). Over the next thirty years, an additional 270,000 women of childbearing age are projected to enter the United States, or approximately 9,000 per year—an annual increase of .02 percent (U.S. Bureau of the Census, 1996b). Their impact may be higher than these numbers suggest. The majority of new immigrants are from Mexico and other Latin American nations (U.S. Immigration and Naturalization Service, 1996), and women of Hispanic origin in the United States as a group have significantly higher birth rates than non-Hispanic women (Ventura and others, 1996).

Although some areas of the nation are significantly affected by international immigration, the overall impact of immigration on the U.S. population is nominal in comparison to the impact of natural increase (births over deaths). Increases in births are the single greatest source of population growth and of projected increase in demand for educational services. Between 1975 and 1990, the number of babies born per year increased approximately 32 percent, an average of about 2 percent per year. The number of babies born in the United States surpassed four million babies per year in 1989, peaking at 4.16 million births in 1990, just 3 percent short of the 4.27 million births reached in 1961 at the height of the postwar baby boom. Since 1990, the number of births per year has declined slowly, to approximately 3.9 million births per year in 1995 (see Figure 1.1) (Ventura and others, 1996, p. 28).

Much of the increase in births during this period can be attributed to an increase in the birth rate for women born at the peak of the postwar baby boom (1946 to 1964), a significant portion of whom delayed child rearing. Birth rates for women in their thirties increased almost continuously in the 1980s and more rapidly than for most other age groups (Ventura and others, 1996). For that reason, the upswing in births during the 1980s is often referred to as the baby boom echo.

As the baby boom echo reaches school age between 1995 and the year 2000, many of the nation's school systems will be stretched to their limits. According to figures released by the National Center for Education Statistics, elementary and secondary enrollments reached a new record in fall 1996 with 51.7 million children. Moreover, this represents only "the mid-point of a 20-year trend of rising school enrollments. By the year 2006, America's schools

Figure 1.1. Births in the United States, 1960 to 1995

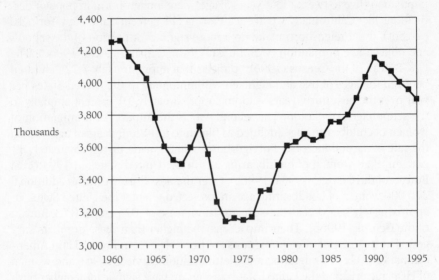

Sources: Ventura and others, 1996, p. 28; National Center for Health Statistics, 1996, p. 1.

will have to educate 54.6 million children—almost 3 million more than today (U.S. Department of Education, 1996b, p. 2)." High-growth states, such as Nevada, California, and Texas, are already resorting to portable classrooms and double sessions to deal with overcrowded schools (U.S. Department of Education, 1996b).

The baby boom echo will result in a 20 percent increase in the number of high school graduates between 1995 and 2005 (U.S. Department of Education, 1995b; Western Interstate Commission for Higher Education [WICHE], 1993a). Because high school completion rates are currently higher than in the 1970s, at the peak of the baby boom echo, the public high school graduating class of 2008 is projected to exceed 3.1 million students, 7 percent more than graduated at the height of the postwar baby boom in 1979 (Western Interstate Commission for Higher Education, 1993a, p. 8).

A dramatic increase in the size of the traditional college-age population is inevitable. However, several factors may militate against a parallel increase in college enrollments. First, the composition of the baby boom–echo generation is different from previous generations. A more substantial percentage of this cohort is composed of racial and ethnic groups that traditionally have low high school completion rates and have been underrepresented in higher education. Second, the projected decline in the size of the twenty-five- to thirty-five-year-old population is likely to result in a comparable decline in higher education enrollments for that age group. This may slow overall growth in higher education enrollments.

From Minority to Majority

The U.S. Bureau of the Census (1993) estimates that by the year 2000, more than one-third of the school-age population will be African American, Asian-Pacific Islander, American Indian-Alaskan Native, or Latino. Statistics on changes in the racial-ethnic composition of elementary and secondary enrollments and of high school graduates further illustrate this shift. Nonwhites and Latinos made up an estimated 28 percent of the nation's high school graduating class in 1995, compared with only 22 percent of the class of 1986. Latinos were estimated to increase from 6 percent of high school graduates in 1986 to around 9 percent in 1995, and Asians-Pacific Islanders were estimated to increase from 2.6 percent of graduates in 1986 to approximately 4 percent in 1995 (Western Interstate Commission for Higher Education, 1993b).

States in the South and West are being affected the most by these changes. In 1995, more than 30 percent of high school graduates were nonwhite or Latino in fifteen states, including all eleven states along the southern border of the United States from California to North Carolina (see Figure 1.2). As early as 1989, the high school graduating classes in Hawaii, New Mexico, and the District of Columbia were more than one-half nonwhite and Latino. By 1995, two additional states, California and Mississippi, were projected to have no single racial-ethnic majority in their high school graduating classes (Western Interstate Commission for Higher Education, 1993b).

If nonwhite and Latino students graduated from high school at the same rate as whites, they would make up roughly 30 percent (versus 28 percent) of all graduates in 1995.[4] However, high school completion rates for Latinos and African Americans are significantly lower than for whites. Only 8 percent of white non-Latino eighth graders in 1988 failed to receive a diploma or its equivalent four years later, compared with 15 percent of African Americans, 18 percent of Latinos, and 25 percent of American Indians-Alaskan Natives. Asians-Pacific Islanders had the lowest overall dropout rate, 4 percent (U.S. Department of Education, 1996a, table 10).[5]

Not only do Latinos, American Indians-Alaskan Natives, and African Americans graduate from high school at a lower rate, they also do not enroll in undergraduate programs at the same rate as whites. Although college-going rates for white non-Latino youth have increased during the past twenty years, college-going rates for Latinos and African Americans have not increased significantly. In 1994, 64 percent of white high school graduates, compared with 49 percent of recent Latino and 51 percent of African American high school graduates, were enrolled in postsecondary education (U.S. Department of Education, 1995a, p. 187). Sample sizes for American Indians-Alaskan Natives and Asians-Pacific Islanders are too small to calculate college-going rates for these groups.

Unless disparities in college-going rates across racial and ethnic groups decrease, the net effect is likely to be a smaller increase in college enrollments than would be expected from the increase in the overall college-age population. If current college-going rates remain unchanged between now and 2005,

Figure 1.2. Nonwhite and Latino High School Graduates, 1995 (Projected)

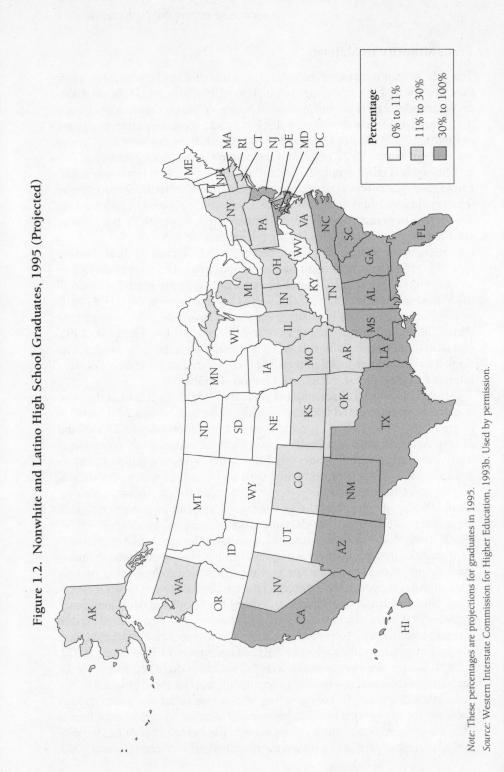

Percentage

0% to 11%

11% to 30%

30% to 100%

Note: These percentages are projections for graduates in 1995.

Source: Western Interstate Commission for Higher Education, 1993b. Used by permission.

a projected 11 percent increase in eighteen to twenty-four-year-olds will translate into a 10 percent increase in college enrollments, or approximately 1.6 million additional students (U.S. Bureau of the Census, 1993; U.S. Department of Education, 1995a, p. 187). In contrast, if all racial and ethnic groups in 2005 were to attend college at the rate whites do today, this increase would jump to 18 percent, amounting to an additional 2.7 million students (U.S. Bureau of the Census, 1993; U.S. Department of Education, 1995a, p. 187).

Mature Students

In the 1980s, increases in the enrollment of students over the age of twenty-four in higher education helped offset declines in the eighteen- to twenty-four-year-old population. In 1993, students over the age of twenty-four made up 44 percent of total enrollments and 37 percent of undergraduate enrollments. Of undergraduates over twenty-four years of age that year, more than half (55 percent) were between the ages of twenty-five and thirty-four (U.S. Department of Education, 1995a).

As we enter the twenty-first century, mature students will continue to be an important part of higher education, but they are not likely to be as large a part as they were in the 1980s and early 1990s. The National Center for Education Statistics projects that college enrollments of those over age twenty-four will remain stable at approximately 6.5 million between 1995 and 2005 (U.S. Department of Education, 1995b, p. 14). The twenty-five to thirty-four age group is expected to shrink almost 12 percent during this period. Fortunately, this decline will be offset by a sizable increase in the forty- to forty-four-year-old age group—15 percent from 1995 to 2005 (U.S. Bureau of the Census, 1993). Nevertheless, because the size of the traditional college-age population is increasing at the same time, the proportion of mature college students is projected to decline from 44 percent in 1993 to 40 percent in 2005.

However, sheer numbers may not be the only factor affecting the enrollment of the over twenty-four-year age group. With larger percentages of the population finishing more of their education before the age of twenty-five, we might expect that college-going rates for the over twenty-four-year-old population will decline. In fact, fewer students are delaying enrollment in college. When the peak of the postwar baby boom left high school in 1979, about 49 percent of recent high school graduates enrolled immediately in college. In 1994, approximately 62 percent of graduates enrolled in college the following fall (U.S. Department of Education, 1995a, p. 187). Moreover, in 1994, more than one-third (35 percent) of all eighteen to twenty-four-year-olds were enrolled in college, compared to only one-quarter of eighteen to twenty-four-year-olds in 1979 (U.S. Department of Education, 1995a, p. 189). Not only are more youths enrolling in college, but more of the overall population is completing four years of college. In 1980, only 17 percent of persons age twenty-five and over had completed four or more years of college, but by 1994, that figure had increased to 22.2 percent (U.S. Department of Education, 1995a, p. 17).

On the other hand, there are other reasons to believe the college-going rate for persons over age twenty-four will not decline. First, the college-going rate for persons twenty-four and over has not changed significantly since 1975. It has remained stable at 10 percent of those twenty-five to twenty-nine years of age and 6 percent of those thirty to thirty-five years of age (U.S. Department of Education, 1995a, p. 15). Second, the pool of persons over age twenty-four who are eligible for higher education is increasing. More youths than ever before are completing four years of high school. Only 68.6 percent of persons over twenty-five years of age had finished four or more years of high school in 1980, compared with 80.9 percent in 1994 (U.S. Department of Education, 1995a, p. 17). These factors, coupled with job insecurity and greater demand for retraining in today's economy, may actually lead to an increased demand for higher education among those over the age of twenty-four.

What Lies Ahead: College Enrollments in the Twenty-First Century

As the size of the college-age population increases and the over twenty-four-year-old population stabilizes, what will happen to higher education enrollments? Midrange projections produced by the National Center for Education Statistics estimate a 6 percent increase in total college enrollments between 1995 and 2005 (U.S. Department of Education, 1995b, p. 26). These projections are based on the assumption that college-going rates for eighteen to twenty-four-year-olds will continue to increase, and the over twenty-four-year-old college-going rate will remain stable. If this assumption is correct, this would bring total enrollments to just over 16 million students in 2005, 918 thousand more students than were enrolled in 1995.

If we assume that the college-going rates of eighteen to twenty-four-year-olds will not be as high as they have been in the 1980s and early 1990s, these midrange estimates may be too large. However, even the National Center for Education Statistics' low-range estimates project enrollment growth from 14.4 million students in 1995 to 15.3 million in 2005, a 5.6 percent increase (U.S. Department of Education, 1995b, p. 26).

Benefits and Burdens: Who Will Be Affected the Most

In the 1970s and 1980s, increases in the percentages of mature and traditionally underrepresented students led to a greater emphasis on part-time enrollments and two-year programs. As we enter the twenty-first century, we might expect that increases in the traditional college-age population would once again shift more attention toward four-year institutions and full-time enrollment. The traditional college-age population of eighteen to twenty-four-year-olds tends to enroll in four-year institutions and attend college full-time. However, the effect that might be expected from an increase in the eighteen- to twenty-four-year-old population is being offset by a substantial increase in the percentage of underserved students. Therefore, very little change is projected in the distribution of enrollments among types of institutions (two- and four-year) or between full- and part-time enrollments. Four-year institutions are expected to maintain a 61 percent share of total enrollments between 1995 and 2005, whereas full-time enrollments are expected to increase only slightly from about 55 percent in 1995 to 57 percent in 2005 (U.S. Department of Education, 1995b, pp. 26–28).

The real shift in higher education enrollments is likely to be geographic. The baby boom echo has not affected all regions or states equally. Nor will the decline in the over twenty-four-year-old population affect all regions or states in the same manner. Unfortunately, there are no consistent, comprehensive, state-level projections for higher education enrollments available. To obtain a sense of how the various regions and states will be affected by the baby boom echo, we must turn to two sources—U.S. Census Bureau projections by age and state and state-level projections of high school graduates.

These projections show that the western states are likely to experience the greatest increases. According to the U.S. Bureau of the Census (1994b), the fifteen- to nineteen-year-old population in the West is projected to increase approximately 27 percent between 1995 and 2005. This demographic surge underlies projected increases in the number of high school graduates in the region of approximately 34 percent, from almost 550,000 graduates in 1995 to more than 730,000 in 2005 (Western Interstate Commission for Higher Education, 1993a, p. 13). Historically, the West has had the smallest graduating classes in the nation. However, around the year 2005, the West will surpass the Midwest and Northeast and will graduate more youth from its high schools than any other region except the South (Western Interstate Commission for Higher Education, 1993a). The West also will not experience as large a decline in the over twenty-four-year-old population as other parts of the country. The twenty-five- to thirty-four-year-old population is expected to decrease only 5 percent in the West between 1995 and 2005 (U.S. Bureau of the Census, 1994b).

In contrast, the Northeast and Midwest are not likely to experience significant population increases. Their young adult populations are projected to increase modestly, 17 and 10 percent respectively, between 1995 and 2005 (U.S. Bureau of the Census, 1994b). Consequently, high school graduates in these regions also are projected to increase modestly, 16 percent in the Northeast and 8 percent in the Midwest (Western Interstate Commission for Higher Education, 1993a). However, the twenty-five- to thirty-four-year-old populations in both regions are projected to decline significantly between 1995 and 2005, 22 percent in the Northeast and 12 percent in the Midwest (U.S. Bureau of the Census, 1994b).

The South will experience moderate changes in both populations. The fifteen- to nineteen-year-old population in the South is expected to increase by about 17 percent, whereas the twenty-five- to thirty-four-year-old population is projected to increase by 10 percent (U.S. Bureau of the Census, 1994b).

Some states in the South are among the fastest growing. Florida, for example, is expecting an increase of more than 50 percent in its high school graduates, followed by Georgia, Virginia, and Texas, which are expecting increases of 20 percent or more over this period (Western Interstate Commission for Higher Education, 1993a). The South will remain the single largest producer of high school graduates well into the twenty-first century (Western Interstate Commission for Higher Education, 1993a).

Migration

If institutions of higher education in the Northeast and Midwest are going to benefit from the baby boom–echo generation's demand for higher education, they will need to recruit students from other regions of the country, primarily from the West and the South. However, several factors may militate against a massive redistribution of students.

First, college student migration has remained at a fairly constant rate for the past two decades. Approximately 20 percent, or one in five, freshmen choose to leave their home states to attend college in another state (Mortenson, 1996, p. 2). This does not mean that states cannot successfully recruit out-of-state students. Massachusetts recruited more than twenty-two thousand students from other states in 1994, leaving it with a net in-migration of more than ten thousand first-year students (U.S. Department of Education, 1994).

Second, most freshmen who migrate tend to stay close to home. More than one-half of those students who migrate from a state in the West migrate to another state in that region (Western Interstate Commission for Higher Education, 1995a). If this holds true for students in the South, it will be difficult for states with declining or stable populations to attract a large number of students from these regions.

Birth and Fortune: Is Demography Destiny?

Enrollment forecasting is, arguably, one of the most important jobs at a state planning agency, system office, or institution. Enrollment forecasts are used in tuition setting, budget forecasting, staffing decisions, resource allocation decisions, and enrollment management. Although institutional researchers who are responsible for enrollment forecasting are not usually expected to be policy analysts, it is important that they are aware of policy issues that may affect the accuracy of forecasts. Moreover, knowing how policymakers plan to use enrollment forecasts is an important consideration in the institutional researcher's choice of forecasting method.[6]

Simple demographic projections are direct and straightforward and provide a very accurate picture of the population. If more babies are born in 1980 than in 1979, we can safely assume there will be a similar increase in the eighteen-year-old population eighteen years later. However, these projections are misleading as indicators of change in enrollment demand. Changes in demand for postsecondary education depend as much, or more, on college-going rates as on demographics.

We saw in the 1980s that projections applying current college-going rates to the declining college-age population were not accurate predictors of changes in demand. As the size of the college-age population declined, college-going rates increased significantly, offsetting projected decreases in enrollment demand. In fact, Easterlin (1989) argues that projections based on the college-age population and historical college-going rates are systematically biased. He traces historical movements in the college-going rate to illustrate that for every movement, up or down, in the size of college-age populations, there are compensating changes in the college-going rate.

Whether the college-going rate will decline as we enter the twenty-first century to compensate for the expected increase in the college-age population is yet to be seen. The point remains, however, that the most important factor in projecting enrollments in the twenty-first century will be accurate projections of college-going rates.

A number of factors will influence college-going rates as we enter the twenty-first century. First, the college-age student of the twenty-first century is more likely to belong to a racial or ethnic group that traditionally has been clustered among the lower socioeconomic classes of our society and has been less well served by the nation's elementary and secondary schools. To quote Carol Frances (1989), "One of the most important factors in projecting college enrollment in the 1990s will be projection of college-going rates—specifically, projection of the speed at which the gap is closed between the college-going rates of whites and those of disadvantaged minorities." In the absence of aggressive programs to improve academic preparation for college and adequate financial aid programs to enable these students to enroll in higher education, the college-going rate of the baby boom–echo generation may fall short of expectations.

Second, changes in the economy often influence students' decisions about whether or not to attend college. Most statistical models for estimating enrollment demand assume that demand increases as the perceived economic payoff from college attendance rises and decreases when the perceived payoff declines (Leslie and Brinkman, 1988; Clotfelter, Ehrenberg, Getz, and Siegfried, 1991). Therefore, when employment is scarce and the potential for foregone income is low, college-going rates tend to increase. Likewise, when employment opportunities are plentiful, the potential for foregone income is high and college-going rates tend to decline. When the potential for earning a good income without attending college is low, then college-going rates increase (and the converse). As we enter a period of relative economic growth in the late twentieth century, this calculus may be important in determining college-going rates. Although higher education enrollments increased at some colleges and universities in fall 1996, others, particularly public institutions in the

Southwest, have reported unexpected enrollment declines, which have been attributed in part to the existence of "a robust job market" in that region (Geraghty, 1996, p. A46).

Moreover, as the baby boom–echo generation approaches college-going age, it may be met with barriers to access. Between the late 1980s and the mid 1990s, support for higher education declined significantly. Mandates to fund K–12 education, Medicare, and correctional facilities shifted state funding priorities away from higher education. As a consequence, state funding to higher education per full-time equivalent student declined in constant 1994 dollars from a high of $5,193 per student in fiscal year 1987 to a low of $4,387 per student in fiscal year 1994 (Research Associates of Washington, 1994). Higher education responded with both de jure enrollment limitations—higher tuition rates and stricter admission standards (Western Interstate Commission for Higher Education, 1991, 1995b; College Board, 1995)—and de facto enrollment limitations—such as capping institutional enrollments at levels that do not exceed physical plant capacity or acceptable faculty-student ratios (Western Interstate Commission for Higher Education, 1991; California General Assembly, 1996)—any of which may have a negative impact on college-going rates.

California provides one of the most dramatic examples of how college-going rates can be affected by shrinking resources. In the early 1990s, it was projected that California would need to build fifteen to twenty-two new campuses to handle a 40 percent increase in enrollments, or 750,000 new students, by 2005. In the mid 1990s, however, enrollments in California's public institutions declined. Slower than expected population growth accounts for only a portion of the decline. In addition, fee increases of 200 percent or more at some institutions (Western Interstate Commission for Higher Education, 1995b, p. 5), stricter admission standards, and course reductions discouraged students from enrolling at California's public institutions (California General Assembly, 1996). California's college-age population is still expected to grow. However, more recent projections of enrollment demand that take into account lower college-going rates place enrollment growth in California's public institutions of higher education at a significantly lower 450,000 new students (California General Assembly, 1996).

On the other hand, the increasing use of distance-learning technologies targeted at place- and time-bound students may increase college-going rates among some populations. In 1993, only a small percentage of faculty and students were involved in distance-learning courses, 7 percent and 3.5 percent, respectively. However, one-third of the nation's institutions reported in 1993 that they offered credit-granting distance-learning programs (Corporation for Public Broadcasting, 1994). Moreover, efforts such as the Western Governors' University, the new regional distance-learning initiative of the Western Governors' Association, promise to expand educational opportunities significantly for place- and time-bound students by using information technology to cross state and institutional lines.

Conclusion

A dramatic increase in the pool of college-age students in the next twenty years is inevitable, but this will not necessarily lead to dramatic increases in higher education enrollment. The correlation between increases in the young adult population and higher education enrollments is not direct. Past experience shows that numerous variables determine whether different populations will take advantage of higher education. Accurate forecasts of enrollment demand must take all of these variables into account, and institutional researchers must be ready to employ methodologies that make it possible to compare the effects of different environmental factors and public policies on enrollments. Enrollment forecasters are obligated to ask how economic growth, an increase in tuition, or an increase in Scholastic Assessment Test requirements will affect demand and to be clear about the assumptions they are making about future college-going rates.

For higher education enrollments, demographics are not destiny. The baby boom–echo generation, much like the postwar–baby boom generation before it, may make its presence felt in almost every aspect of American life. However, it is not inevitable that this generation will enroll in higher education at numbers comparable to their presence in the population. The choices we make as a society, not demographics, will determine if this generation will enjoy the same levels of educational attainment previous generations enjoyed.

Notes

1. *Baby boom echo* is the name demographers have given to the children of the postwar–baby boom generation. The image of a tidal wave has sometimes been used to describe the effect the postwar–baby boom generation has had on the nation's resources. Some authors have chosen to invoke this image again by referring to the baby boom–echo generation as *tidal wave II* (Kerr, 1994).

2. The surge of immigration in the 1980s and early 1990s represents a recent high point. Immigration to the United States declined more than 20 percent between 1993 and 1995 (U.S. Immigration and Naturalization Service, 1996).

3. The figures from the U.S. Bureau of the Census (1996a, 1996b) on international immigration used here include counts of legal immigrants, refugee immigrants, and an estimate for undocumented immigrants.

4. The assumption is that if high school graduation rates were the same for all racial and ethnic groups, the distribution of high school graduates by race would be equal to the distribution of six-year-olds twelve years earlier in 1983 (U.S. Bureau of the Census, 1990).

5. We should not assume from these figures that all Asians-Pacific Islanders have high educational attainment rates. Educational attainment varies considerably across various Asian ethnic groups. Moreover, the Asian-Pacific Islander subpopulations with the highest educational attainment rates (Japanese, Chinese, and Filipino Americans) are declining in population relative to more recent immigrant populations (such as Vietnamese, Laotians, and Kampucheans) that have lower educational attainment rates (Gardner, Robey, and Smith, 1985).

6. For additional information, see Chapter Five on enrollment-forecasting techniques by Brinkman and McIntyre.

References

California General Assembly. *Projections and Prophecies: Planning for the Enrollment Tidal Wave*. Sacramento: California General Assembly, 1996.

Clotfelter, C. T., Ehrenberg, R. G., Getz, M., and Siegfried, J. J. *Economic Challenges in Higher Education*. Chicago: University of Chicago Press, 1991.

College Board. *Annual Survey of Colleges*. New York: College Board, 1995.

Corporation for Public Broadcasting. *1994 Study of Communications Technology in Higher Education*. Washington, D.C.: Corporation for Public Broadcasting, 1994.

Easterlin, R. A. "Demography Is Not Destiny in Higher Education." In A. Levine and Associates (eds.), *Shaping Higher Education's Future: Demographic Realities and Opportunities, 1990–2000*. San Francisco: Jossey-Bass, 1989.

Frances, C. "Uses and Misuses of Demographic Projections: Lessons for the 1990s." In A. Levine and Associates (eds.), *Shaping Higher Education's Future: Demographic Realities and Opportunities, 1990–2000*. San Francisco: Jossey-Bass, 1989.

Gardner, R. W., Robey, B., and Smith, P. C. "Asian Americans: Growth, Change, and Diversity." *Population Bulletin*, Oct. 1985, *40* (4), 3–43.

Geraghty, M. "On Campuses Coast to Coast, Trends in Freshman Enrollment Vary Widely This Fall." *Chronicle of Higher Education*, Sept. 20, 1996, p. A46.

Kerr, C. *Preserving the Master Plan*. Sacramento: California Higher Education Policy Center, Oct. 1994.

Leslie, L. L., and Brinkman, P. T. *The Economic Value of Higher Education*. Old Tappan, N.J.: Macmillan, 1988.

Mortenson Research Seminar on Public Policy Analysis of Opportunity for Postsecondary Education. "Trends and Patterns in Interstate Migration of College Freshmen." *Postsecondary Education Opportunity*, Aug. 1996, no. 50.

National Center for Health Statistics. "Births, Marriages, Divorces, and Deaths for 1995." *Monthly Vital Statistics Report*, July 1996, *44* (12).

Research Associates of Washington. *State Profiles: Financing Public Higher Education 1978 to 1994*. (17th ed.) Washington, D.C.: Research Associates of Washington, 1994.

U.S. Bureau of the Census. "United States Population Estimates, by Age, Sex, Race, and Hispanic Origin: 1980 to 1988." *Current Population Reports*. P25–1045. Washington, D.C.: U.S. Government Printing Office, Jan. 1990.

U.S. Bureau of the Census, by Day, J. C. "Population Projections of the United States, by Age, Sex, Race, and Hispanic Origin: 1993 to 2050." *Current Population Reports*. P25–1104. Washington, D.C.: U.S. Government Printing Office, Nov. 1993.

U.S. Bureau of the Census. "The Foreign-Born Population, 1994." *Current Population Reports*. P20–486. Washington, D.C.: U.S. Government Printing Office, Mar. 1994a.

U.S. Bureau of the Census, by Campbell, P. R. "Population Projections for States by Age, Sex, Race, and Hispanic Origin: 1993 to 2020." *Current Population Reports*. P25–1111. Washington, D.C.: U.S. Government Printing Office, Mar. 1994b.

U.S. Bureau of the Census, Population Estimates Program, Population Division, ST-96–3. *Estimates of the Population of States: Annual Time Series, July 1, 1990 to July 1, 1994 and Demographic Components of Population Change, Annual Time Series, July 1, 1990 to July 1, 1994*. Washington, D.C.: U.S. Government Printing Office, 1996a.

U.S. Bureau of the Census, Population Division. "Population Projections of the United States by Age, Sex, Race, and Hispanic Origin: 1995 to 2050." *Current Population Reports*. P25–1130. Washington, D.C.: U.S. Government Printing Office, 1996b.

U.S. Bureau of the Census. *Resident Population of the United States: Estimates by Age and Sex*. Washington, D.C.: U.S. Government Printing Office, 1996c.

U.S. Department of Education. National Center for Education Statistics. Integrated Postsecondary Education Data System. *Fall Enrollment Survey, 1994–95*. Washington, D.C.: U.S. Government Printing Office, 1994.

U.S. Department of Education. National Center for Education Statistics 95–029. *Digest of Education Statistics*. Washington, D.C.: U.S. Government Printing Office, 1995a.

U.S. Department of Education. National Center for Education Statistics 95–169. *Projections of Education Statistics to 2005*. Washington, D.C.: U.S. Government Printing Office, 1995b.

U.S. Department of Education. National Center for Education Statistics. *Dropout Rates in the United States: 1994*. Washington, D.C.: U.S. Government Printing Office, 1996a.

U.S. Department of Education. *NCES—A Back to School Special Report: The Baby Boom Echo.* Washington, D.C.: U.S. Government Printing Office, 1996b.

U.S. Immigration and Naturalization Service. *Immigration Fact Sheet*. Washington, D.C.: U.S. Government Printing Office, Aug. 1996.

Ventura, S., and others. "Advance Report of Final Natality Statistics 1994." In National Center for Health Statistics, *Monthly Vital Statistics Report,* Supplement, June 24, 1996, *44* (11).

Western Interstate Commission for Higher Education. "Enrollment Limits: A Response to Quality and Financial Concerns in Higher Education." *WICHE Reports on Higher Education in the West*. Boulder, Colo.: Western Interstate Commission for Higher Education, 1991.

Western Interstate Commission for Higher Education. *High School Graduates: Projections by State, 1992 to 2009*. Boulder, Colo.: Western Interstate Commission for Higher Education, 1993a.

Western Interstate Commission for Higher Education. *The Road to College: Educational Progress by Race and Ethnicity*. Boulder, Colo.: Western Interstate Commission for Higher Education, 1993b.

Western Interstate Commission for Higher Education. "College Student Migration." *WICHE Policy Insights*. Boulder, Colo.: Western Interstate Commission for Higher Education, 1995a.

Western Interstate Commission for Higher Education. *Tuition, Fees and Financial Aid in Public Higher Education in the West, 1995–96 Detailed Tuition and Fee Tables*. Boulder, Colo.: Western Interstate Commission for Higher Education, 1995b.

ROBIN ETTER ZÚÑIGA *is research associate with the Western Interstate Commission for Higher Education in Boulder, Colorado.*

This chapter examines the major trends and issues in the financing of American higher education in the 1990s, including the diversity of issues facing different types of institutions.

Financing American Higher Education in the 1990s

Arthur M. Hauptman

In the mid 1990s, American higher education became a $200 billion enterprise. The activities financed by this $200 billion are tremendously diverse, ranging from huge research universities with budgets of several hundred million dollars to small liberal arts colleges with budgets of several million dollars.

This chapter addresses four aspects of how American higher education is financed in the 1990s. First, it examines trends in the overall level of resources devoted to the enterprise. Second, it discusses the current level of dependence on, and trends in, the major revenue sources. Third, it analyzes the changing role of the various financial aid programs in helping students and their families pay for college. Finally, it identifies the critical financial challenges facing different sectors and types of institutions. In each instance, the chapter speculates on future financial trends.

Overall Level of Resources

By most reasonable standards, America has the best-funded system of higher education in the world. Spending by American colleges and universities in the mid 1990s accounted for nearly 3 percent of the Gross Domestic Product (GDP) (U.S. Department of Education, 1996c; U.S. Government, 1995).[1] This is a higher percentage of GDP devoted to higher education than in any other country in the world. It also represents a tripling over the past half century in the proportion of GDP devoted to higher education (see Figure 2.1).

Much of the growth in higher education's share of the American economy comes from the increased proportion of the population enrolled in college.

Figure 2.1. Higher Education Spending as a Percentage of Gross Domestic Product

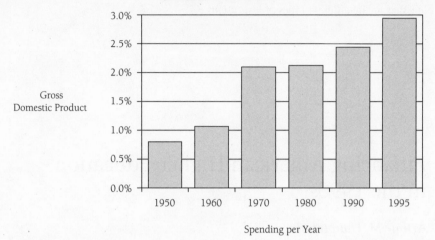

Sources: U.S. Department of Education, 1996c, Table 166, p. 175; U.S. Government, 1995, Table B-1, p. 274.

Like the proportion of GDP devoted to higher education, the proportion of the population sixteen years of age and older enrolled at any one time in higher education also has tripled over the past half century (see Figure 2.2).

The increase in the proportion of the economy devoted to higher education, however, reflects more than just increased participation. Spending per student has also grown in real terms over time, doubling over the past half century (see Figure 2.3) and increasing by roughly 25 percent when adjusted for inflation over the past fifteen years.

Overall economic growth will be a key determinant of how fast resources for higher education grow in the future. Based on historical experience and simulations, strong economic growth in the range of 2 to 3 percent real growth per year is likely to produce substantial increases in resource levels for higher education in the future.

The simulations indicate that this growth in higher education resources will occur even if the proportion of federal and state taxpayer dollars devoted to higher education declines and even if public confidence in higher education in the future is low. (For a discussion of such simulations, see Hauptman, 1992).

On the other hand, low or negative rates of economic growth will most likely result in declining resources per student even if public confidence is high and a larger share of public dollars goes to higher education. In effect, within foreseeable levels of economic growth, the overall size of the economic pie is more important to future resource levels for higher education than is the specific slice of that pie that higher education receives.

Figure 2.2. Percentage of the Population Enrolled in Higher Education

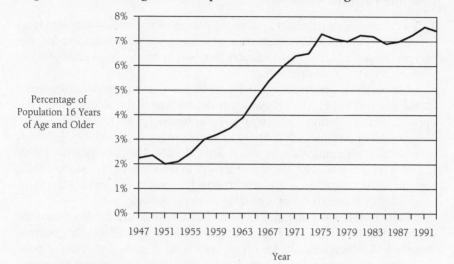

Percentage of
Population 16 Years
of Age and Older

Year

Sources: U.S. Department of Education, 1996c, p. 176; U.S. Government, 1995, p. 312.

Figure 2.3. Spending per Student in Real Terms Since 1950

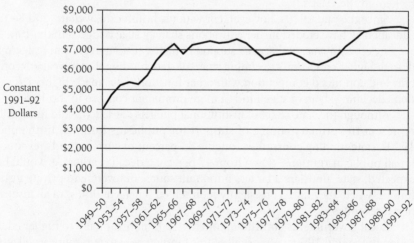

Constant
1991–92
Dollars

Academic Year

Source: U.S. Department of Education, 1996c.

Revenue Patterns

This section reviews trends in four major sources of revenues—state and local funding, the federal government, tuitions and fees, and endowment income and private giving. Table 2.1 indicates trends in revenues from each of these sources in the 1980s and 1990s.

Each of the major revenue sources for higher education grew substantially in real terms in the 1980s. This was particularly true in the second half of the decade when a growing economy proved to be a boon for higher education. This growth in revenues contributed to a sense of financial well-being, which surrounded higher education for much of the decade. The pattern in the 1990s has been far different, with the rate of growth in resources often less than inflation. In some instances, actual declines in funding in current dollars have replaced previous patterns of growth in constant dollars.

State and Local Financial Commitment.   States are the largest source of governmental funding for higher education. In the mid 1990s, they provide roughly $45 billion annually for higher education in general support of public institutions, state student aid programs, and a host of categorical programs.

For most of the past half century, overall state funding of higher education has grown much faster than inflation to support growing enrollments and demands for more services. One notable exception to this trend was the first several years of the 1990s when state spending for higher education stalled and actually fell in current dollars for the first time since these statistics began to be kept in the 1950s.

Since the mid 1970s, however, corrections, health care, welfare, and K–12 education all have eroded higher education's share of state budgets. In the 1980s, a strong economy meant that state support of higher education grew in real terms despite higher education's declining share of state funding. But a weaker economy and continued competition with other functions have made higher education's declining share of state funds a more prominent concern in the 1990s.

Although the state share of institutional budgets has fallen, state funds still represent the primary source of support for public institutions. In the mid 1990s, state funding constitutes roughly 35 percent of current funds revenues for all public institutions, down from 45 percent a decade earlier. As would be expected, state funds are a far less important source of revenue to private institutions, where they have consistently represented 3 percent or less of all institutional revenues.

Local governments contribute roughly $5 billion annually to higher education in the mid 1990s. Almost all of this funding goes to community colleges where local tax dollars typically represent between one-quarter and one-half of current fund revenues. By contrast, local tax dollars represent less than 5 percent of revenues at public four-year institutions, and are an insignificant source of revenue for private institutions.

A growing issue for private institutions is whether they make payments to the community in which they are located in lieu of the taxes they do not pay

Table 2.1. Trends in Major Revenue Sources Since 1980

Revenue Source	Dollars in Billions				Percentage Change		
	1980–81	1985–86	1990–91	1995–96 (est.)	1980–81/ 1985–86	1985–86/ 1990–91	1990–91/ 1995–96
Tuition and fees	13	23	37	55	77	61	49
Federal government	10	13	18	22	30	38	22
State and local government	21	32	43	49	52	34	14
Endowments/gifts	5	8	12	17	60	50	42
Sales and services	14	24	40	50	71	67	25
Other sources	2	3	5	7	50	67	40
Total current fund revenues	65	103	155	200	58	50	29
Inflation rate					31	21	17

as a result of their tax-exempt status. This issue of tax exemption and pay-ments-in-lieu-of-tax is a hot one in many communities, particularly in light of several recent court rulings that suggest private colleges should lose their tax-exempt status if they fail to meet certain criteria.

Federal Funding.   The federal role in higher education serves three major purposes. First, the federal government sponsors a wide variety of student aid programs, consisting of grants, loans, and work-study, which provide more than two-thirds of all aid available in the mid 1990s. Second, the federal government is the primary funder of university-based research, providing as much as three-fourths of all funding for this purpose. Third, it supports institutions through a wide variety of categorical programs.

For all these functions, the federal government spends about $25 billion annually on higher education in the mid 1990s, excluding any tax breaks that relate in various ways to higher education expenses. Thus, the federal government spends roughly half of what state and local governments spend on higher education. Roughly half of the $25 billion annual federal commitment to higher education is devoted to the various federal student aid programs.

Measuring the federal presence in student aid and the financing of higher education can be confusing, however. One source of confusion is that the face value of federal student loans does not appear on the federal budget; instead, only the subsidies, default payments, and administrative costs associated with these loans are budgetary items.[2] Thus, the more than $10 billion that the federal government annually spends on student aid in the mid 1990s leverages more than $30 billion in financial aid that is provided to students.

It is also difficult to measure precisely the size of federal student aid relative to institutional budgets because most of the aid does not appear in statistical reports as a federal revenue to institutions. Instead, these funds appear as part of the tuition and fees or room and board items that the aid supports.

Student Charges.   Tuitions and other student charges in both the public and private sectors have increased at roughly double the rate of inflation for the past fifteen years. Although the annual percentage growth in student charges has slowed in the mid 1990s from previous patterns, it still is roughly double the rate of inflation.

Although the overall percentage growth in tuition and fees has been similar between the two sectors, the patterns and the reasons for this growth have been distinctly different. Tuitions continue to be the principal source of revenue for private institutions. In the mid 1990s, they account for roughly two-fifths of all current funds revenues of private institutions, a proportion that has remained largely the same over the past several decades. Tuitions and other charges at private institutions tend to increase faster during times of economic prosperity, when colleges believe their students and their families can afford the higher rates of increase, and when the costs of various factors of production including faculty, staff, and utilities tend to increase at faster rates than during recessions.

By contrast, tuitions at public institutions tend to increase faster during times of economic recession, as states have more difficulty in maintaining their financial commitment to public institutions because of shortfalls in tax revenues. As state funds become more constrained, tuitions are increased to make up for the shortfalls. As a result, tuitions as a share of all revenues have grown at public institutions. In the mid 1990s, tuition and fees represent about one-fifth of total revenues at public institutions, up from less than one-sixth a decade earlier.

The growth in public sector tuitions is largely a function of state funding patterns. When the economy is strong, and state revenues are growing, the growth in public sector tuitions and fees tends to be relatively moderate. During recessions, when state tax revenues flag, tuitions increase more to make up for the shortfall in state revenues. Thus, public sector tuitions tend to increase the most when students and their families can least afford to pay them.

The growth in tuitions and fees in both the public and private sectors over the past decade and a half mirrors the tremendous growth in the college wage premium—the difference between what college graduates earn and what those without a degree earn. In the 1990s, the college wage premium is at its highest level ever, and many in higher education point to the growth in the college wage premium as a principal argument for the need to send more students to college (U.S. Department of Education, 1996c).[3]

But this emphasis on the private benefits of higher education may undercut arguments for greater public support. It also may be short-lived, as the college wage premium is cyclical depending on a number of economic and demographic trends. For example, if more people graduate from college in the future, the college wage premium could decrease as labor-market shortages shift.

Endowment Income and Private Giving.   The size of endowments and the strength of alumni and other private giving are among the most distinctive features of American higher education. This reliance on private giving, in addition to tuitions, represents a primary reason that America devotes such a high proportion of its economy to higher education, as most countries rely much more on public resources to fund their higher education systems.

Private giving has been a particularly important revenue source for independent institutions, where endowment income and private gifts on average represent 10 to 15 percent of total revenues. Contrary to the common perception, however, most private colleges do not have substantial endowments. Roughly one hundred private institutions have endowments with market values in excess of $100 million; endowments of the remaining fifteen hundred private institutions are much smaller.

Nonetheless, for many private colleges, fundraising has long represented the critical ingredient that allows them to be independent of government and to stay in business. Without this source of funds, most private institutions would either have to come under the aegis of state governments or would be forced to charge substantially higher tuitions than they do.

Fundraising is increasingly part of the responsibilities of public sector officials as their institutions seek to replace shortfalls in state funding and reduce the need to raise tuitions. The most notable trend in this regard is the growth of foundations at public colleges and universities, which typically operate separately from the institution itself. But national statistics on public colleges and universities do not accurately reflect this important trend because foundation activities typically are not included in data reported by institutions.

Changing Role of Student Aid in Paying for College

Over the past three decades, student aid, especially loans, has become increasingly prominent in the financing of American higher education. In 1995–96, roughly $50 billion in student financial aid was provided in all forms from federal, state, institutional, and private sources. (See College Board, 1996, for information on student financial aid presented throughout this chapter.) More than four-fifths of this total aid was provided to students enrolled in higher education institutions; the remainder was for students enrolled in trade schools and other forms of short-term training programs that are not included in the higher education statistics. The $40 billion in federal aid represents roughly two-fifths of the estimated $100 billion in total costs of attendance that college students faced in the 1995–96 academic year.

The growth over time in the overall amount of student aid available consists of mixed trends in the three major forms of student aid—need-based grants, loans, and work-study.

Need-Based Grants.   Need-based grants initially were the primary form of student financial assistance. In the past two decades, however, grants have been replaced by loans as the principal source of aid. The federal Pell Grant program is by far the largest government-sponsored grant program, spending about $6 billion annually in the mid 1990s. This level of spending represents more than a doubling in real terms over the level two decades earlier.

Despite this real increase in funding, the buying power of Pell Grants has not increased over this time, for several reasons. First, as already mentioned, college tuitions and other charges have increased substantially faster than inflation since 1980, thereby negating the effect of increased federal spending for Pell Grants. Second, the number of Pell Grant recipients has also grown since the mid 1970s, thereby reducing the growth in per-recipient award levels. Third, the mix of aided students has changed over time, with lower-income students representing an increasing proportion of Pell Grant recipients. As a result of these different factors, the maximum Pell Grant award has declined when adjusted for inflation over the same time period that overall funding level for the program has increased in constant dollars.

The other principal federal grant program, Supplemental Educational Opportunity Grants, has not enjoyed as much of an increase as Pell Grants, its younger counterpart. What the program receives in annual appropriations in the mid 1990s is about one-tenth of what the Pell Grants program now receives and is roughly the same in real terms as what it received in the mid 1970s.

Student Loans.   Loans over the past two decades have become a major source of financing higher education. In the mid 1990s, they represent more than half of the total amount of financial aid, compared to one-fifth or less two decades ago. Total borrowing for college now reaches $30 billion annually. Loans now finance roughly one-third of total charges for college tuition, fees, room, and board, up from less than one-tenth two decades ago (see Figure 2.4).

This increased reliance on loans has raised a number of worrisome consequences. First, more borrowing by students represents a generational shift in responsibilities from parents to their children. Second, although there are no conclusive data, many fear that the growth in indebtedness may adversely restrict student choices of the colleges they attend and the careers they enter. Third, the huge increase in student indebtedness may serve as a major obstacle to how much many institutions can charge in the future.

For many years, most borrowing was by students enrolled in either independent or proprietary institutions. One of the most marked developments in the past decade, however, is that borrowing is much more prevalent among students enrolled in public sector institutions than used to be the case. For example, students at public four-year institutions now borrow roughly one half of all subsidized student loans, up from one-third a decade ago.

Students in public sector institutions also represent a large share of the borrowers in the unsubsidized loan program that was authorized in 1992, partially a function of middle-income students not qualifying for subsidized loans because of the lower costs of attendance in that sector. Similarly, a recent survey indicates that roughly one-half of all baccalaureate recipients borrow, regardless of whether they graduate from a public or private institution.

College Work-Study.   The federal College Work-Study program regularly is cited as among the most effective student aid programs, because students

Figure 2.4. Percentage of Tuition, Fees, Room, and Board Financed by Loans

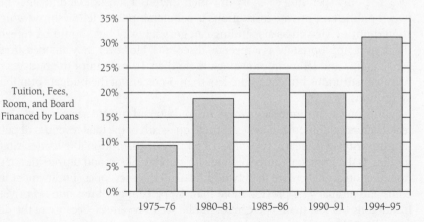

Tuition, Fees, Room, and Board Financed by Loans

Year

Source: College Board, 1996.

have to earn the benefit rather than being given money in the form of grants or borrowing with the possibility of default. Yet, the roughly three quarters of a billion dollars that the federal work-study program receives in appropriations in the mid 1990s is roughly one-quarter less in real terms than what the program received in federal appropriations two decades ago.

Issues Facing Different Sectors or Types of Institutions

The preceding discussion does not take into account one of the fundamental facts of higher education in America, namely, that the financial condition of different types of institutions and the challenges they face in the years ahead vary substantially. This final section identifies some of the major financial issues and challenges faced by public and independent institutions as well as those faced by four major types of institutions—research universities, comprehensive universities, liberal arts colleges, and community colleges.

Principal Issues Facing Public and Private Institutions

Public and private institutions tend to be far more similar in their expenditure patterns than in their revenues (U.S. Department of Education, 1996b;[4] McPherson and Schapiro, 1994). For example, instruction constitutes between one-quarter to one-third of the total budget in both the public and private sectors, research accounts for between 5 and 10 percent of total spending, and public service represents less than 5 percent of total spending in both types of institutions. Operation and maintenance of plant represent about 7 percent of total spending for both public and private institutions, student services represent about 5 percent of the budget in both types of institutions, and academic support activities account for between 6 to 7 percent of total spending in both sectors.

The only spending category in which there is a substantial difference between public and private institutions is scholarships and fellowships (which should not be viewed as a spending category anyway but should be categorized more appropriately as a revenue discount). However they are measured, scholarships and fellowships average more than 10 percent of the budgets of private institutions but constitute less than 5 percent of the budgets of public institutions.

It is on the revenue side where the public and private sectors have their real differences. Tuition and fees constitute one-sixth of the total revenues of public institutions but nearly two-fifths of all private institutional revenues. State funding is the principal source of funds for public colleges and universities, representing on average more than two-fifths of all their revenues. Endowment income and annual gifts provide more than 10 percent of all revenues of private institutions but less than 5 percent of public sector revenues. Because of the differences in their structures and in their principal sources of funds, public and private institutions tend to face distinctly different sets of financial issues.

Changing Patterns of State Support.   The principal financial issue facing public colleges and universities in this country is how much support they will receive from state governments in the future and whether the rules and formulas that govern how states allocate funds to institutions will change in light of changing demographic and economic factors.

One concern about public colleges and universities, which is very much related to the more limited funding they now receive from states, is the increased *time-to-degree* for their undergraduates, who on average now take in excess of five years to graduate. This increase in time-to-degree may in part be a function of restricted state funding, which, when it leads to enrollment caps in many states and fewer course offerings at many public institutions, limits the ability of students to enroll in the courses they need to graduate.

The fact that tuitions are rising rapidly at many public colleges at the same time that students are frozen out of classes and taking longer to complete their degrees does not help the public's perception of public higher education. Unlike public institutions, where lengthening in the time-to-degree is a major concern, private colleges' average time-to-degree has not changed materially over time.

Private college officials have a keen interest in how states finance public institutions, although they are less directly affected by this source of support than their public counterparts. Their biggest worry in this regard is that public institutions, by virtue of their state subsidy, are able to charge a much lower price than private institutions, placing them at a competitive disadvantage.

Growing Gap Between Resources and Expectations.   All colleges and universities are faced with rising expectations in the form of growing numbers of students and families believing that higher education is the principal ticket to success in our society and worrying that they will not be able to buy that ticket. This growth in expectations is fueled by such demographic factors as the projected increase in the number of high school graduates, which confirm that the demand for higher education will increase rapidly for the foreseeable future.

Public institutions will tend to bear the brunt of these rising expectations, as historical trends indicate that most of the new students who aspire to higher education will enroll in public institutions. In addition, in most of the southern and western states, where the demand for college will be greatest, a relatively large share of college students are enrolled in public institutions.

Private college officials face a slightly different problem in this regard. Unlike their public sector counterparts, they are not expected to educate most of the growing numbers of students for whom higher education previously was an impossible dream. The private college "problem" is mostly one born of the perception of having inadequate resources at the same time that the tuitions they charge are reaching once unimaginable heights. It is this juxtaposition of high prices and nice facilities on the one hand and claims of poverty on the other that poses one of the biggest public relations challenges for private institutions in this country.

Limits of High Tuition–High Aid. The most fundamental financial issue facing the broad range of private colleges and universities in this country is whether they are approaching or have exceeded the limits of the "high tuition–high aid" strategy that served them so well in the 1980s. Most private colleges raised their tuitions much faster than inflation in the 1980s and reinvested an increasing percentage of these tuition dollars in financial aid. The concept underlying this effort was to increase resource levels while at the same time increasing the diversity of their student bodies through the aggressive use of student aid discounts. For most institutions, this strategy worked well in the 1980s.

Whether most private institutions can continue with this high tuition–high aid strategy is a real question. First, there is growing consumer resistance to further steep tuition hikes after more than a decade of rapid increases. Second, as a higher proportion of students are aided, a smaller proportion of each additional tuition dollar is available for purposes other than student aid, unless institutions abandon need-based aid policies.

The dilemma that many private colleges are now facing can be summarized by the following question: Is it possible to increase tuitions, improve diversity, and prevent the exodus of middle-class students, yet still have enough money left over from student aid requirements to pay for program and facility improvements? The answer in the 1980s seemed to be yes for most institutions. With higher charges and more aid recipients in the 1990s, however, the answer now for most private colleges seems to be no.

Interestingly, as many private colleges are questioning the viability of the high tuition–high aid strategy, more and more states and public institutions are debating whether such an approach makes sense for them. Many public institutions now find themselves in a position similar to that which faced private institutions in the early 1980s—they are charging tuitions that are far less than what many of their students would be willing to pay to attend. Not surprisingly, therefore, a number of states and individual public institutions are borrowing from the private college model and using a high tuition–high aid strategy as a means for dealing with shortfalls in state funding for higher education.

Issues Facing Different Types of Institutions

As many differences as there are in the financial challenges facing public and private institutions, the real diversity in the financial issues that colleges and universities face and in their economic situations emerges when different types of institutions are examined. The following discussion focuses on the principal financial issues faced by four types of institutions—research universities, in both the public and private sectors; comprehensive institutions; private liberal arts colleges; and community colleges. Collectively, these four types of institutions account for four-fifths or more of all higher education enrollments in the United States.

Research Universities. Over the past half century, federal support of campus-based research has become a critical component of financing research universities in this country. Federal grants and contracts now account for roughly one-fifth of all revenues for these institutions in both the public and private sectors; the bulk of this support is for campus-based research activities. This degree of dependence on federal funds defines a set of issues that research universities face related to the receipt and use of these funds.

One such issue is the continuing set of controversies related to indirect cost recovery, including what costs are legitimately regarded as being part of research activities. Another issue is the inadequacy of research facilities, which previously were funded separately by the federal government but now are essentially financed out of the indirect cost pool. The pattern of federal research funding over time—for example, the changing mix of defense- and non-defense-related research—is still another issue in this area.

Whereas all institutions must grapple with achieving an appropriate balance between teaching, research, and service, a research university is the type of institution where these tensions are most pronounced. This level of tension means that research universities must periodically address the question of how to ensure that undergraduate education receives the appropriate amount of attention in institutional discussions, policies, and budgets.

In addition, the complexity of research universities has also become a financial issue for these institutions as they have grown in the scope and diversity of activities for which they are responsible. These are big organizations, with annual budgets that often exceed $100 million, and with many constituencies and complex management problems that often include running large health care facilities, big-time athletic programs, and large physical plants that may cover many square miles, not to mention the challenging job of educating thousands of students. The task of running organizations like this should not be minimized in considering the issues facing them.

Comprehensive Institutions.   Possibly the single most important issue facing comprehensive institutions is the pressure they face to become research universities. This pressure becomes an issue because typically these institutions lack the resources to make this transition successfully. For every comprehensive that succeeds in becoming a research-oriented institution, many more fail and end up with strained budgets and disgruntled students who worry about what kind of education they are receiving.

A comprehensive also is the type of institution that will feel the greatest pressure to accommodate the growing numbers of students who will be coming out of high school seeking a baccalaureate. To the extent that sufficient funds are not likely to be provided for this purpose, however, these institutions will face a large task.

To the extent that faculty shortages emerge or worsen in certain fields of study in the future, comprehensive institutions are most likely to feel the impact. Research universities and premier liberal arts colleges are now, and are likely to remain, the institutions most successful in attracting new faculty talent. They will also be most able to recruit existing faculty to fill whatever gaps exist in the future mix of their faculties. The result of these flows of new and existing faculty will be that any faculty shortages will have the most impact at the comprehensive institutions.

For several reasons, comprehensive universities also may be most affected by the application of technology and telecommunications to learning processes, particularly through distance learning. First, they are the public institutions that are most likely to have a mismatch between growing demand and inadequate resources and thus may be most interested in exploiting technology. Second, these institutions serve a higher proportion of more nontraditional students than other four-year institutions. These are the students who are more likely to be interested in the possibility of distance learning in the home than students of more traditional college age. Third, comprehensive institutions tend to be more flexible and more attuned to market forces than research universities and liberal arts colleges and therefore may be more willing to experiment with technological applications to learning.

Liberal Arts Colleges.   One of the most noticeable trends in American higher education in recent decades has been a growing vocationalism in which students view the value of the education and the degree they receive as directly connected to the jobs they get once they graduate. Liberal arts colleges more than any other type of institution seem to be swimming against this tide of vocationalism by insisting on the intrinsic value of a liberal education (Breneman, 1994).

The critical and distinctive essence of liberal arts colleges is their small size, small classes, heavy interaction between faculty and students, and a streak of independence from political forces. These strengths, however, also may represent the Achilles' heel of these institutions. Many liberal arts colleges lack the critical mass and resource base to withstand external shocks as well as competition for their best students from research universities and public comprehensive institutions. These institutions face the issue of whether they can maintain or add quality to their programs without ruining their ability to compete with less expensive alternatives.

A liberal arts college also is the type of higher education institution that seems most subject to competitive pressures of various kinds. One such pressure is from peer colleges, which often are competing for the same pool of students. This competition for students involves a wide range of institutional policies, including tuition setting; student financial aid; the quality of academic, dormitory, and recreational facilities; and amenities, among others.

Another competitive pressure for liberal arts colleges comes from public institutions, which can offer their programs at a fraction of what private institutions charge because of the large state subsidies they receive. It is this competition from public universities that seems to most engage many private college officials when they are asked about the pressures their institutions face.

These competitive pressures—with other private colleges and with the public sector—relate to the basic financial calculus that most private colleges, but especially liberal arts colleges, must solve. One equation in this calculus is how to maintain or add to the quality of programs and services without reaching beyond the ability of the market to pay for them. A second equation is how to cut costs without affecting quality. These are tough questions that liberal arts college officials regularly must address.

Community Colleges.   Most community colleges rely heavily on local property taxes as a primary source of support; these revenues typically pay for one-quarter or more of a community college's budget. Over the past several decades, local property taxes have come under attack for a number of reasons, including charges of regressivity and unfairness in their application. Local taxes have also been the subject of a number of state tax-cutting initiatives, referenda, and legislation. Continued taxpayer resistance to property and other local tax sources could spell big trouble for community colleges, which rely so much on these sources of revenues.

Although community colleges are rightly regarded as one of the great success stories of American higher education, two persistent concerns about them are their low graduation rates and low levels of articulation with four-year colleges. Though many students enroll in community colleges for purposes other than receiving a degree or transferring to a four-year institution, the rate at which community college students either complete their programs or transfer is very low. This lack of success undercuts the credibility of community colleges as academic institutions and therefore could reduce their future levels of public and private financial support.

Because their mission is so fundamentally tied to the goal of providing access, community colleges provide a disproportionate share of the growing amount of remediation that American higher education institutions are being asked to provide to correct inadequate preparation of students in elementary and secondary education. One of the financial issues associated with remediation is that, typically, the institutions that provide it are not adequately compensated for the costs of providing it. Thus, the institution always feels behind to the extent that its revenues do not meet the costs associated with remediation. A related issue is that loans are being used to finance much of remedial education. To the extent that many of the students who take remedial courses will not be able to pay off their loans, we as a society are consigning them to a future of being bad credit risks and a permanent burden to society.

A community colleges is also the type of institution that is most involved with the provision of vocational training for specific job-related skills. This involvement in vocational training raises a number of related financial issues. One such issue is the keen competition that community colleges face from proprietary trade schools, which offer programs that provide many of the same sets of skills as community college training programs.

Competition and cooperation with businesses is another issue raised by the degree to which vocational training is offered by community colleges. Many community colleges have come to rely on the revenues from their programs that provide training for the employees of local businesses on a contract basis. But to the extent that businesses become dissatisfied with the performance of the community college and seek alternative providers or decide to train their own employees, the financial foundation of the community colleges erodes.

The considerable overlap that exists between education and training programs at both the federal and state levels is still another issue related to the vocational training that community colleges provide. The confusion that is created by this overlap, and the lack of a systematic approach for financing short-term vocational training, may be contributing to the fact that America lags behind many other industrialized countries in developing specific skills geared to the needs of the workplace.

Importance of Institutional Research

This chapter has been drawn with a broad brush, aimed at providing the big picture of how higher education is financed in America in the 1990s. Although institutional researchers focus on the financing and the demographics of a particular institution, the trends and issues presented in this chapter provide a context for understanding the issues that individual institutions face.

What states are doing, how the federal role in higher education may be changing, overall trends in giving, and the degree to which financial aid is being provided and in what forms are all considerations within which institutional plans must be realized.

As this chapter has also indicated, these overall trends will have different implications for different institutions. A factor that may be critically important for one type of institution may be largely irrelevant for another. To be successful, the plans of each institution must incorporate consideration of overall trends as well as the issues facing particular types of institutions.

Notes

1. Spending and revenue figures for higher education in this chapter are from the U.S. Department of Education's *Digest of Education Statistics* (1996c). The data source for national economic activity, population trends, and price indices is the U.S. Government, *Economic Report of the President, 1995*.

2. Further adding to the confusion, with recent changes in federal budget rules, the annual federal costs of student loans are now estimated on a *present value basis;* that is, the flow of costs are estimated over the life of the loan and discounted back to their present value, whereas spending for grants and other forms of aid continues to be shown on an annual basis.

3. Because of data limitations, the college wage premium is typically calculated by comparing the annual earnings of individuals with differing levels of education. The primary data source is U.S. Department of Commerce, Bureau of the Census, *Current Population Reports*. These data are summarized in the U.S. Department of Education's *Condition of Education* (1996a). In the mid 1990s, wage and salary workers twenty-five to thirty-four years old with four or more years of college had more than twice the earnings of individuals who did not complete high school. For males, this wage differential was only 50 percent in the 1970s when there was considerable discussion of people being overeducated.

4. Data for different spending categories come from U.S. Department of Education, National Center for Education Statistics, *Current Funds Revenues and Expenditures of Institutions of Higher Education* (1996b).

References

Breneman, D. *Liberal Arts Colleges: Thriving, Surviving, or Endangered?* Washington, D.C.: Brookings Institution, 1994.

College Board. *Trends in Student Aid.* Washington, D.C.: College Board, 1996.

Hauptman, A. M. *The Economic Prospects for American Higher Education.* Washington, D.C.: Association of Governing Boards of Universities and Colleges and the American Council on Education, 1992.

McPherson, M., and Schapiro, M. "Expenditures and Revenues in American Higher Education." Williamstown, Mass.: Williams Project on the Economics of Higher Education, Sept. 1994.

U.S. Department of Education, National Center for Education Statistics. *Condition of Education.* Washington, D.C.: U.S. Government Printing Office, 1996a.

U.S. Department of Education, National Center for Education Statistics. *Current Funds, Revenues and Expenditures of Institutions of Higher Education.* Washington, D.C.: U.S. Government Printing Office, 1996b.

U.S. Department of Education, National Center for Education Statistics. *Digest of Education Statistics.* Washington, D.C.: U.S. Government Printing Office, 1996c.

U.S. Government, President's Council of Advisers. *Economic Report of the President.* Washington, D.C.: U.S. Government Printing Office, 1995.

ARTHUR M. HAUPTMAN is an independent consultant specializing in higher education finance and public policy issues. He is a senior fellow with the Association of Governing Boards.

Enrollment management planning at the statewide level requires the coordination and analysis of many variables. It is important to have policies and ongoing planning efforts in place to react to changes in the higher education marketplace. This chapter provides a case study of enrollment management planning in the University of Wisconsin System.

Enrollment Management in a Statewide System of Public Higher Education: A Case Study

Nathan D. Peters, Sue L. Keihn

The University of Wisconsin System (UW System) is currently in the third phase of systemwide multiyear enrollment management planning. The first phase of current enrollment management planning began in the UW System in 1985 when the board of regents undertook a comprehensive strategic planning effort, *Planning the Future,* which established Enrollment Management I (EM I), effective for years 1987–1990. Subsequently, a second plan, Enrollment Management II (EM II), effective for years 1991–1994, and a third plan, Enrollment Management III (EM III), have been developed, which authorize enrollment targets through the year 2000. This chapter summarizes the various plans, reviews what other states are doing regarding statewide enrollment management, and outlines the demand and supply variables taken into consideration for the UW System's most current enrollment plan. The policy objectives of the planning, the change in process as enrollment planning progressed through the various phases, and the outcomes—both expected and unexpected—are also discussed.

Background

The UW System was created in the early 1970s through a merger of the University of Wisconsin and the Wisconsin State Universities. It is governed by a seventeen-member board of regents appointed by the governor. The UW System is composed of twenty-six campuses—two doctoral-research campuses, eleven regional comprehensive campuses offering bachelor's and master's degrees, thirteen two-year campuses, and a statewide extension with offices in all seventy-two

Wisconsin counties. There are 150,000 full- and part-time students—or 123,600 full-time–equivalent enrollment (FTE). Of these students, 122,000 are state residents, and 28,000 are from out of state or from other countries.

The UW System includes all public universities in the state. Additional opportunities for postsecondary education include the independent private colleges and universities and the Wisconsin State Technical College System.

The budget of the UW System totals $2.5 billion, with approximately twenty-eight thousand staff positions (ten thousand connected with instruction). The UW System ranks in the top ten for enrollment and total budget for multicampus public higher education systems (National Association of System Heads, 1994). State dollars constitute 34 percent ($840 million) of this total, down from 50 percent at the time of merger. This change reflects the shift from a state-supported to a state-assisted university. Wisconsin is considered a low-tuition state, with resident undergraduate students charged $2,650 per academic year at doctoral institutions, $2,100 per academic year at regional comprehensive institutions, and $1,900 per academic year at the two-year campuses. Resident undergraduate tuition covers about one-third of a student's total instructional costs.

Summary of Enrollment Management I and II Plans

Enrollment Management was first endorsed by the UW System's board of regents in 1986, when student FTE and head count had grown to an all-time high. Unplanned enrollment increases stretched fiscal and staff resources as state support per student was $4,200 (for all thirteen four-year institutions), $1,200 below the national average of $5,400. Furthermore, overall support per student declined in inflation-adjusted dollars as new dollars from both state and tuition sources could not keep pace with enrollment growth.

FTE enrollment had grown 16 percent (19,510 FTE) from 1973 to 1986 (119,200 FTE to 138,710 FTE). However, during the first half of the 1980s, sixteen hundred fewer class sections were offered by the UW System. Student and parent complaints about access to courses, large class sizes, high student-to-faculty ratios, outdated laboratories and classrooms, extended time-to-degree, erosion of student services, and inadequate instructional material (libraries, computers, and so forth) produced reaction from both the board of regents and state politicians.

These problems were exacerbated by a tuition revenue–management policy that created a short-term incentive for institutions to admit more students than they could absorb fiscally. UW System's tuition revenue policy allowed institutions to keep tuition revenue that was generated from additional enrollment. Because tuition covered only one-third of the cost of each additional student, educational quality, in the long run, could not keep pace with student demand. Under these conditions, tuition revenue could first offset marginal costs of educating students where additional instructional capacity existed, but it fell quite short of meeting students' total costs, as this capacity was depleted at most campuses by the mid 1980s.

As a result of these problems, the board of regents asserted the priority of educational quality over access that initiated EM I (1987–1990) and EM II (1991–1994). Student enrollment subsequently decreased by thirteen thousand FTE. These enrollment management plans were considered a success because state support per student reached the national average, support per student increased in real terms (adjusted for inflation), new freshmen qualifications improved, and—surprisingly—measurable access to the UW System did not decrease. (The reduction in the gaps in support per student between Wisconsin's level and the national average was due in part to reductions of support in other states in the 1990s.) These changes culminated in a reduction of complaints from students and parents, as resources were more appropriately balanced with student supply.

Enrollment reductions and new state dollars funded 341 extra faculty and financial aid positions along with the creation of an ongoing laboratory-, classroom-, and computer-modernization program combined to increase state and overall support per student adjusted for inflation beyond levels that existed in the late 1970s (see Table 3.1). However, these fiscal goals would not have been achieved if solely dependent on new resources. It was enrollment management, which meant fewer students per available dollars, that generated the increases in state and overall support per student in the UW System.

Freshman academic qualifications actually improved during enrollment management. Academic qualifications are measured by high school percentile rank and average class rank. Table 3.2 illustrates this improvement. In addition, average ACT scores of new freshmen remained above national averages.

The UW System defines access as the percentage of immediate Wisconsin high school graduates who enroll in the same year that they graduate from high school. Although access was not an initial focus of early enrollment management planning, access rates increased due to a coinciding demographic decline in the number of high school graduates during this period. The systemwide proportion of Wisconsin high school graduates who enrolled immediately upon high school graduation was maintained between 31 and 33 percent during this period, compared to 25 percent in 1976. This made enrollment management politically feasible, as the UW System was not in a position where it was denying admission to many Wisconsin residents.

Revisions in tuition revenue–management policy also changed institutional philosophies toward meeting enrollment targets. Incentive for institutions to enroll additional students beyond enrollment target levels was eliminated because all tuition revenue was now pooled. Therefore, institutions, whether by design or inaccurate enrollment projections that forced them to miss enrollment targets, did not benefit financially from additional generated revenue. These "excess dollars" generated above budget levels were held as systemwide reserves and used in future years to reduce tuition rate increases.

Table 3.1. Quality Measures for Enrollment Management

	Before Enrollment Management	After Enrollment Management
Support per undergraduate student (adjusted for inflation)	$2,600	$3,000
Gap in national state support per student	$1,200	$0
Average undergraduate class size	30	27
Student-Faculty ratio	19:1	17:1

Table 3.2. Academic Qualifications of University of Wisconsin Freshmen

High School Percentile Rank	Before Enrollment Management	After Enrollment Management
Freshmen in top ten percent	57.8%	59.9%
Freshmen in top quartile	56.3%	60.9%
Freshmen in top half	77.0%	84.0%
Freshmen in bottom quartile	5.8%	2.8%
Average class rank	64.7	69.1

One additional important point to note here is that not all institutions reduced enrollments under these two enrollment management plans. Under EM I, four institutions with excess instructional capacity increased enrollment, whereas for EM II, one institution continued to grow based on an assessment of regional need.

In conclusion, the enrollment management program in the UW System that began in the mid 1980s provided benefits to institutions and students. Institutions benefited from additional resources per student and higher-quality students. Students had improved access to courses and faculty as well as improved instructional and student service resources.

Review of Enrollment Planning in Other States

Only a few states have instituted policies that address enrollment directly. The higher education coordinating board in the State of Washington issued a state master plan in 1987 (Higher Education Coordinating Board, 1987), with a revision in 1996 (Higher Education Coordinating Board, 1996), which includes state enrollment goals. The Washington enrollment goals are for the state to reach the 70th percentile in participation rate for upper-division graduate and professional enrollments by 2020. Lower-division enrollments will continue to maintain the current participation rate. Those actions will increase enrollment by nearly fifty-seven thousand students. The Florida Board of Regents has established a statewide enrollment plan (Keihn, 1996), which governs both enrollment and funding to support enrollment. California's master plan is under current debate (Keihn, 1996) as resources dwindle and demand increases exponentially.

Oregon and New York use recommended funding or tuition levels to control enrollments indirectly. North Carolina, Nevada, and Ohio are in the process of formalizing statewide enrollment management plans (Keihn, 1996). The Georgia Board of Regents adopted the Admissions Policy Direction in 1996, establishing and implementing clear and consistent admissions standards, which are designed to achieve better student success in and access to the university (Georgia Board of Regents, 1996).

Enrollment Management III Plan

EM II ended in 1994–95 along with the decline in the number of Wisconsin high school graduates. Due to a strong economy and existing planning, the UW System was able to plan for the challenges beginning in 1995 and beyond without resorting to crisis management. Under EM III, the goal of enrollment management remained the same as in previous plans—to maintain or increase educational quality. What changed for the UW System was demographic conditions that shifted from a focus on total FTE counts to concentration on both FTE and access for Wisconsin high school graduates, and a reversal in the planning process.

The number of Wisconsin high school graduates peaked in 1977 with a 32 percent decline by 1994. The number of graduates began to increase again in 1995 and will grow by more than forty thousand additional Wisconsin high school graduates over the six-year period of EM III (1995–2001). The trend line of Wisconsin high school graduates shown in Figure 3.1 is very similar to national and other statewide trends. However, the enrollment projections for Wisconsin high school graduates remain relatively stable after the year 2004. Unlike some other states (for example, California and Washington), Wisconsin does not expect continually increasing demand by high school graduates.

Enrollment management planning in the UW System is largely based on immediate high school graduates. For UW System institutions, fully 80 percent of degree-seeking undergraduates enter the UW System as freshmen, constituting 64 percent of all enrollment. Among new freshmen, 73 percent come directly from Wisconsin high schools, 11 percent are Wisconsin high school graduates who enter later, and 16 percent come from other states. The undergraduate student body is only a little older now, on average, than a decade ago, when 85 percent were in the "traditional" age group (twenty-four and younger). This trend echoes demographic changes in the age distribution of the Wisconsin population. Fewer undergraduates in the older age groups (twenty-four and up) were expected, particularly because this younger group (ages eighteen to twenty-four) had participated at higher rates in higher education at a traditional age, and this younger group (ages eighteen to twenty-four) is smaller in number. Enrollment Management I and II had not significantly changed the attendance patterns of Wisconsin high school graduates.

Figure 3.1. Wisconsin High School Graduates, 1976–2004

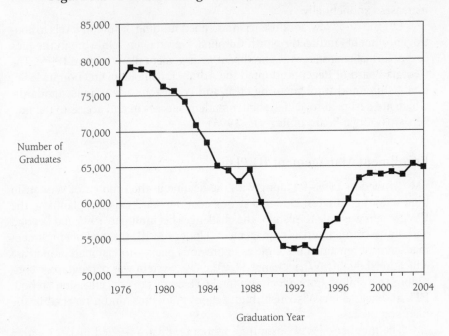

Source: University of Wisconsin System, Office of Policy Analysis and Research.

The UW System ranks in the top five nationally in access rates for immediate high school graduates for public four-year postsecondary education and provides the majority of postsecondary enrollment opportunities in the state for Wisconsin high school graduates. The UW System's access rate is 31 percent, whereas the other two postsecondary enrollment options—Wisconsin Technical College System and Wisconsin Private Colleges and Universities—enroll 13 percent and 7 percent, respectively, of Wisconsin high school graduates.

Planning Process. Prior UW System enrollment management plans were "top-down" approaches with centralized information and planning. There was little opportunity for public input or debate prior to implementation. In addition, these plans were usually followed by board of regents–mandated program reviews and reallocation efforts.

In contrast, EM III was developed in an open and public manner over eighteen months, using institution-based plans, which assumed that institutions would need to be as creative and efficient as possible in using available resources. The board of regents reviewed a series of nine working papers developed by institutional researchers, academic planners, and budget planners on academic and planning issues along with systemwide and regional analysis. These papers focused on topics such as demographics and their implications for planning, overviews of regional and cooperative academic programs, impacts of statewide program and policy initiatives on undergraduate enrollment, number of credits at graduation, and planning partnerships linking systemwide and institutional strategic-planning processes. The board also consulted with demographic experts and conducted two public round table discussions with legislative leaders to discuss goals of enrollment management implementation.

Statewide guidelines for planning recognized the importance of decentralized development to reflect the institutions' abilities to appraise local markets and conditions. Institutional discussions often involved university governance committees, students, administrators, and the community. These institutional efforts were further supported by central office staff visiting each institution to discuss local, regional, and statewide demographics and student demand. The outcome of this planning was the development of enrollment plans for each institution.

Assumptions for Enrollment Projection Planning. Within the development of individual institutional plans, the following set of assumptions were used in institutional enrollment–projection models:

No erosion of quality gains made from the previous two enrollment management plans would be allowed to occur. Some capacity existed to meet demand before adding resources to institution budgets.
No change in continuation rates for students would occur until the year 2000. The proportion of nonresident students enrolled in the system would remain at current levels.
A slight increase in graduate enrollments would occur reflecting state needs.
No change in enrollment shares would occur for Wisconsin private institutions or technical colleges.

Accommodating Additional Students. The EM III plans submitted by UW System institutions identified a total increase of ten thousand student FTE by the year 2000. Based on the assumptions cited above, this level of FTE growth maintained the existing access rate for Wisconsin high school students.

Demographic data showed clearly that the UW System would face an influx of students during this period. Therefore, two planning strategies were needed. First, the UW System had to determine how many more students it would be willing to enroll. Second, an approach was needed to provide the state with clear choices for enrollment access. To assist in focusing the debate, the board of regents developed fifteen assumptions and policy principles to guide EM III planning development. Two principles specifically related to this policy choice. Both principles reaffirmed the board's commitment to maintaining educational quality (if necessary, at the expense of access), and at the same time directing the UW System to customize growth to the needs of each region and recognizing that some growth could be accommodated through existing base resources.

Variable Enrollment Growth. The first of these enrollment management principles states: "The University of Wisconsin will approve variations in enrollment increases across the system, expanding campus enrollments most at those institutions that demonstrate themselves best able to take increases at the most reasonable cost, at no loss of quality and in keeping with their institutional missions and objectives, or where program strengths, along with state needs, are sufficiently compelling" (University of Wisconsin System, 1994, p. 29).

Institutions were asked to develop plans that took their cost structures, any areas of existing capacity, staffing patterns, and program mix into account while maintaining a commitment to serve as many students as possible consistent with their high level of educational quality. Because the plans were institution based and dependent on institutional priorities and resources, variable enrollment growth was expected and even encouraged.

Following the principle above, enrollment growth varied by institution. The average growth for the system was 6.8 percent over 1994 target levels. Enrollment increases for the fourteen institutions ranged from a low of 3.8 percent to a high of 15.1 percent for the six-year period. Six institutions proposed plans with more than double-digit increases; two institutions submitted plans above 15 percent growth. This variation reflected regional needs, institutional mission, and assessment of optimal institutional size.

For example, several institutions had larger-than-expected growth due to the desire to serve nontraditional students. Small institutions wanted larger growth to take advantage of potential economies of scale. Other institutions found themselves in regions with faster-growing populations. Others had only limited capacity to grow in certain programs and thereby limited their enrollment projections.

Cost Structure.   A second principle continued the focus of planning at the individual institutional level while looking at costs for accommodating students:

> The University of Wisconsin System will maintain and enhance the gains made in the quality of undergraduate education under Enrollment Management I and II. A proportion of projected enrollment demand will be accommodated without additional resources by continuing to improve the effectiveness of its administrative, student services, and academic operations through improved efficiency, restructuring, strategic curricular design, and pedagogical innovation, thereby allowing some enrollment growth at no additional cost. Such incremental demand will be met through such efficiencies only when educational quality is not jeopardized. Additional students will then be served if further resources are provided by the state. If enrollment growth has to be limited, this will be accomplished through more selective admission standards. When faced with a choice between maintaining educational quality within budgetary constraints or providing access for students, the priority will be on quality (University of Wisconsin System, 1994).

Based on the above principle, institutions developed enrollment plans identifying additional student FTE in two categories that reflected the probable fiscal reality that the state would not be willing, or able, to fund fully all enrollment growth.

The first category consisted of additional students who would be enrolled without new state resources and without losing the benefits accrued through previous enrollment management and other strategic-planning efforts. These FTE were also dependent on the state's commitment to continue funding certain university costs, such as utilities, debt service, fringe benefits, and so forth, and no budget reductions.

The second category referred to additional students who would be enrolled only if additional state support was provided.

Using the ten thousand FTE in institutional enrollment plans, these FTE were divided into *four thousand FTE* that could be accommodated without additional state resources because of the smaller freshman classes from EM I and EM II progressing through institutions, a reduction in the number of credits taken, the use of new instructional technologies, and other available institutional resources including increases in faculty workload and *six thousand FTE* that would require varying levels of new state support.

Institution plans also varied in terms of required additional state support for enrollment growth beyond those accommodated through the UW System's own resources. For example, the enrollment plan for two-year institutions focused on increased retention of sophomore classes in addition to maintaining their share of immediate high school graduates. To improve freshman-to-sophomore retention, additional supplies and expenses and advisory staff were needed. Because space was available in sophomore-level courses, there was also available instructional capacity. However, funding for additional freshman students where campuses were at full capacity required new instruction resources too.

Other plans were tied to specific higher-cost programs, such as allied health, nursing, and agriculture, in which growth reflected student demand and meeting state needs.

Finally, several institutions developed plans that were tied to new capital facility needs. Enrollment growth at two institutions required the construction of new student residence facilities to accommodate additional students. In addition, one institution planned on a new academic building to accommodate growth. One institution received state approval for a new residence hall, and the remaining two capital projects await state authorization.

Policy Objectives.   The three major policy objectives emphasized in EM III were quality, access, and partnership with the state. They reflected the change in fiscal environment, demographics, and locus of decision authority.

Quality.   A major change in UW System outlook was the way two major indicators of educational quality in prior enrollment management plans were treated. Reductions in the student-to-faculty ratio and increases in support per student—major educational success measures of EM I and EM II—were no longer major objectives of EM III.

Reduction in student-to-faculty ratio was an expected outcome under both EM I and EM II. This measure was a major indicator of educational quality and an argument used in obtaining additional state support and faculty positions in the late 1980s. At the start of EM I, the systemwide student-to-faculty ratio was nineteen to one. A systemwide seventeen to one student-to-faculty ratio goal was chosen based on the late 1970s, a time when students were able to get needed classes and when complaints from students and families concerning educational quality were minimal. This goal was reached again during EM II as a result of decreasing enrollment. However, as institutions agreed to increase enrollment without additional state support under EM III, this measure was withdrawn as a quality measure at the request of institutions arguing that it did not represent the complex nature of instruction.

In addition, increasing support per student was also downplayed as a quality indicator in EM III. Similar to what would happen to student-to-faculty ratios, as the number of students increased without commensurate increases in inputs (in this example, dollars), support per student would have to decrease. This was an implicit assumption of EM III as even FTE supported by additional state dollars would not provide enough funding to maintain the current support per student.

However, both of these educational quality measures were assumed to be replaced by increases in the use of technology and quality measurement through new *accountability indicators*. The use of technology in the classroom provided opportunities to teach more students (both on campus and place bound) and to teach them better, as such tools could accommodate different student learning styles and abilities. However, technological innovation was predicated on its availability to both faculty and students. As a result, it was understood that increased technology utilization, which would benefit all students, would require modest up-front investments by the UW System and the state.

The measurable outcomes for improvements in educational quality became eighteen accountability indicators that were jointly developed with legislative staff and the governor's office. These eighteen indicators reflected traditional educational inputs such as dollars spent on instruction, faculty instructional workload, research funding, and outcomes such as graduation and retention rates; sophomore competency testing; minority faculty–recruitment measures; and satisfaction surveys with students, alumni, and employers. These indicators are shared annually with UW System stakeholders. This began the transition, moving away from the more traditional and limited quality indicators to broader-based outcome measures. Furthermore, institutions developed individualized accountability indicators to measure their own specific improvements in educational quality.

Access. The structure of the plan provided a clear public policy choice for state policymakers on what would be the optimal size of the UW System and whether to maintain the 31 percent access rate to meet state higher educational and economic development needs. Only by providing additional state support would the UW System guarantee the 31 percent access rate.

However, the UW System did commit itself to providing additional access through adaptation of distance learning, increases in faculty workload, and through reductions in the total number of credits students complete prior to graduation. Analysis found that the UW System average for baccalaureate graduates was 145 attempted credits compared to a minimum systemwide 128-credit requirement. Further analysis of baccalaureate degree graduates who started in the system as new freshmen found that choice of major was the leading factor in excess credits-to-degree. For example, graduates in the engineering, math, and education fields averaged over 150 attempted credits versus those in the humanities averaging 129 credits. Nonresident students averaged fewer attempted credits at graduation (128) than did resident students (147). Some argued that the difference in attempted credits reflected a nonresident tuition that was three times greater than resident tuition and provided fiscal incentive for these students to limit the number of credits taken. Academic ability, as measured by grade point average (GPA), and whether a student transferred between institutions also were contributing factors to more credits at graduation. Students with higher GPAs had fewer credits at graduation. Transfers had higher than average credits at graduation.

By developing strategies to reduce the average attempted credits at graduation, some institutions projected that they would be able to serve more students during EM III. An approach used by several institutions to accommodate students without additional resources was to develop strategies to reduce credits taken by students. Possible strategies included reducing baccalaureate credits to 120 in all programs, improving advising, and facilitating transfer through expanded articulation agreements. Enrollment projections modeling the attrition and flow of students through the UW System showed that fifteen hundred of the four thousand FTE could be accommodated through effective reduction in credits-to-degree over the period of EM III.

Partnership. The EM III plan was also designed to strengthen the partnership between the state and the UW System and to increase collaborative efforts within the system. The first step in reinforcing the partnership with the state was the UW System's commitment to accommodating 40 percent (four thousand FTE) of the plan's proposed ten thousand FTE increase with its own resources. The plan also stressed quality undergraduate teaching as the UW System's main priority, which was clearly the choice of the public and state leadership. However, the UW System still committed institutions to continuing their involvement in basic and applied research and public service activities, which were important to other state stakeholders and state economic development needs. Finally, the UW System was willing to support other state educational initiatives, such as Tech Prep and School-to-Work, which required additional cooperation among the university, the Wisconsin Technical College System, and K–12 school districts to provide additional educational options for Wisconsin students.

Additional partnership was also bolstered through Partners in the Process, an approach to increase the link between institution and systemwide strategic planning to maximize the benefits of working within a system. This was intended to ensure that statewide issues would be addressed but would reflect the individuality and missions of each institution. The system office would assist in the identification of issues, provide information, serve as a facilitator or coordinator of institution responses, and spot potential areas of collaboration. Institutions would respond to identified issues using their specific planning processes that reflect their own institutional cultures. Areas for future study included improvements in learning, program array, collaborative opportunities, and institutional organization.

Current State of the Plan

Almost immediately after approval of the plan in May 1994 by the board of regents, legislative action doomed implementation. The legislature enacted a major property tax–relief measure that required the state to pay for two-thirds of K–12 public school costs. This imposed an immediate $1 billion commitment of state funds from the upcoming biennial budget, as these costs were a political "first draw" on the state treasury. This shift in state budget priority made it very unlikely that the UW System would receive new funding for additional enrollment or any other fiscal need. This was despite economic forecasts that indicated Wisconsin was in excellent fiscal shape. In contrast, the specter of large state budget reductions for the UW System loomed ahead.

The end result for the UW System was a net reduction of $33 million in state support for the biennium and the loss of over five hundred staff positions. It was the first biennium since the merger of the two systems that the UW System received an absolute reduction in state support after increases for such standard items as compensation and utilities. (Note that the UW System's share of state resources has declined from 14.4 percent of the state budget at merger to less than 10 percent today.) However, the question of whether the UW System would still commit to the additional four thousand students was superseded by an unexpected reduction in enrollment.

For the first time since systemwide enrollment management began in 1987, enrollments fell more than 1 percent below the UW System enrollment management target in fall 1995 (twenty-nine hundred FTE below target), leaving additional capacity in almost all UW System institutions. The decline was unexpected but not unlike enrollment trends nationally. Graduate student enrollments were lower than expected at the major research universities. Transfer students from the two-year UW System campuses were down as was overall enrollment in the two-year campuses.

Analyses indicated that there was no single factor contributing to these unexpected declines in enrollments. The graduating high school class size was actually the largest in several years. The number of immediate high school graduates going to the UW System remained at a similar percentage rate as in preceding years. The retention rate of continuing students was less than previous years and followed a declining trend at nearly every academic level— freshman to sophomore, sophomore to junior, and junior to senior. The decline in continuation rate for previously enrolled students did not exhibit any single characteristic. Students not returning included those with both high

GPA and low GPA, declared majors and nondeclared majors. The strong Wisconsin economy was also believed to be a factor, as jobs were available for students leaving the UW System. This unexpected reduction in enrollment meant that the UW System now needed to be in a position to serve the twenty-nine hundred FTE unserved students from fall 1995 and to accommodate the remaining growth projected during EM III.

In the new state fiscal environment (with expectations of additional federal budget reductions), the board of regents initiated a new study that was not intended as a comprehensive strategic plan but was focused on fine-tuning current policy (including EM III) and practice to enhance the performance of the UW System in the twenty-first century. This ten-month long public study included all board of regents members, UW System chancellors and vice chancellors, central office staff, and representatives from the public, the faculty, the academic staff, and the students; it reaffirmed the board's commitment to educational quality and the original EM III plan and outlined specific obligations for the UW System.

First, despite state budget reductions, the study continued the UW System's commitment to increasing enrollment by four thousand students, but this pledge was dependent on future state action regarding increased management flexibility, stable base funding, and new state investments in technology. Second, instructional technology and distance education were placed in the forefront for improved student-centered learning and supporting additional student access. Third, to assist in meeting the access needs of the state, more emphasis was placed on getting students to graduate faster to free up instructional capacity. These plans included the development of four-year graduation contracts; incentives and disincentives for students to reduce average credits taken, such as reduced state support for credits taken beyond a specified threshold; improved advising and course availability; facilitation of transfer; and increased collaboration with high schools to allow qualified high school students to acquire college credits. Fourth, partnerships within the UW System, as well as with K–12 school districts, Wisconsin Technical Colleges, other governmental agencies, and the private sector, needed more development to promote the pooling of resources and expertise to increase efficiency and improve service to all UW System customers. Finally, in an effort to take into account the overall productivity of the UW System and to shift accountability measurement from inputs to outcomes, the study adopted a concept called *institutional effectiveness,* which considers all resources available to the UW System to meet the needs of students and identify benefits accrued to students as a result of a UW System education.

Implications for Statewide Enrollment Planning

Statewide enrollment planning is essential with the onset of collaboration, educational technology that knows no boundaries, and reduced resources for postsecondary education. To make the most effective use of current resources, higher education at the public and state level must provide stakeholders with a coordinated plan as enrollment planning has budgetary implications.

The three-phase fourteen-year enrollment planning process at the UW System reflects the need for flexibility in approach and changes in goals when enrollment planning is done over several years. The economic, political, and demographic environments can change rather rapidly. Statewide enrollment planning must react to those changes. Therefore, this planning requires a periodic review process and wide dissemination. Finally, planning must also be broad-based and inclusive to generate wide support.

Implications for Institutional Researchers

The changing nature of student behavior, political demands for resources, and institutional versus statewide analysis requires that institutional researchers will need to examine continually the environment, student data, costs, and revenues. The complexity of enrollment planning at the statewide level requires not only the review of policy impact at the statewide and institutional levels but also the interplay between those two levels. For example, UW System tuition set at the statewide level has a trickle-down effect for all postsecondary institutions regardless of whether they are affected directly by the tuition-setting process. Statewide trend data often mask the differences between postsecondary sectors or specific institutions. Institutional researchers must be careful in drawing conclusions based on only one level of analysis.

References

Georgia Board of Regents. "Recommendations on Implementing the Admissions Policy Direction." Report to the Board of Regents of the University System of Georgia, Atlanta, May 8, 1996.

Higher Education Coordinating Board. *Building a System . . . to Be Among the Best . . . The Washington State Master Plan for Higher Education.* Olympia, Wash.: Higher Education Coordinating Board, 1987.

Higher Education Coordinating Board. *The Challenge for Higher Education, 1996 State of Washington Master Plan for Higher Education.* Olympia, Wash.: Higher Education Coordinating Board, 1996.

Keihn, S. [keihns@ccmail.uwsa.edu.] "Survey of State Higher Education Executive Officers." State Enrollment Management Plans, May 1996.

National Association of System Heads. *Multi-Campus Systems of Public Higher Education in the United States: 1994.* Albany, N.Y.: National Association of System Heads, Sept. 1994.

University of Wisconsin System. *Enrollment Management III: Final Plan.* Madison: University of Wisconsin System, May 1994.

NATHAN D. PETERS is assistant vice president for budget planning for the University of Wisconsin System.

SUE L. KEIHN is associate provost for student services and dean of students at the University of Wisconsin-Green Bay.

Private institutions face unique challenges in providing predictability for budgeting and resource deployment.

Enrollment Forecasting and Revenue Implications for Private Colleges and Universities

James H. Day

As the turn of the century approaches, the nation's first and oldest higher education system faces a set of conditions that resemble those of the first half of the twentieth century more than those associated with the periods ushered in by the GI Bill following World War II or the Higher Education Act of 1965. Government grant assistance for students represents a minimal percentage of revenue for most private institutions, which are again dependent on the ability of families to pay or finance tuition. Unlike the first half of the century, however, a much smaller percentage of families are able to pay fully today's tuition rates.

Prior to these landmarks of public policy for higher education, private colleges and universities charged the tuition necessary to generate the revenue and enrollment required to operate their academic programs. In general, these tuition rates were affordable for the growing middle-income population of the country. Public institutions had not yet begun their massive postwar enrollment expansion; their similarity to private liberal arts colleges was reflected in frequent athletic contests in which state schools and private liberal arts colleges were athletic peers. Indeed, most small, private liberal arts colleges can reflect on victories as recently as the 1940s over state schools that are National Collegiate Athletic Association Division I athletic powers today.

The limited scholarship aid that was available to private college students at that time was financed largely by private donors and was administered without the benefit of a formal needs analysis. Scholarships largely went to academically worthy students who could not otherwise afford to attend. Private colleges and universities of the day were largely cash businesses; the notion of a generally available financial aid program, much less the idea of aid as a discount to tuition, is a modern concept.

Since World War II, increased participation in postsecondary education generally has been fueled by demographic factors, such as the earnings premium associated with educational attainment, and by higher education finance policy. Census figures for 1995 indicate that average income for a household headed by a baccalaureate degree holder is $73,334, compared to $43,182 for a household headed by a someone with a high school diploma.

Federal and state need-based grant aid and loans, the extension of the GI Bill, and increased tuition subsidies in the public sector also have contributed to the high level of higher education participation we see today.

This combination of public policies created a new set of economic realities for private colleges and universities. With increased federal grants and loans available to families, as well as state-funded financial aid that could be used at private colleges in some cases, private sector institutions expanded and diversified their student populations. Although still largely dependent on tuition, these institutions and their students could count on a significant share of that tuition to be financed by government sources.

Increased participation by middle- and lower-income families using the help of federal and state financial aid led to increased enrollments and revenues. Freed from total reliance on family tuition payments, and with government as a financing partner, independent colleges could raise tuition and strengthen academic programs without reducing demand. In raising tuition away from what the majority of the population could afford to pay out of current income and toward a level that only very affluent families could afford without assistance, private institutions engaged in a progressive or means-tested pricing strategy in which the contribution families made toward the cost of attendance was determined by their financial resources.

Increasingly, private colleges and universities added institutional grant dollars to government aid to broaden and strengthen their applicant pools, increase enrollment, and become more socially and economically diverse. Indeed, through the 1970s, it was possible for the professional associations serving admissions and financial aid officers—the National Association of College Admissions Counselors and the National Association of Student Financial Aid Administrators—to establish a culture and prescribe professional practices that support the concept of need-blind admission coupled with a commitment to meet the full financial need of admitted students. Most colleges and universities embraced these norms.

The revenue growth that resulted from increased enrollment and higher tuition permitted growth in faculty and their salaries. It also increased academic innovation and investment in academic and co-curricular programs, including new initiatives, such as women's or black studies; new student support efforts, such as career development and various counseling services; and new women's intercollegiate athletic programs as mandated by Title 9.

That Was Then, This Is Now

Until the early 1980s, government aid increased and family incomes grew along with tuition. As a result, private colleges and universities in general did not suffer badly in their competition against the highly subsidized public sector, though their market share was deteriorating, and middle- and upper-income families were moving gradually toward the public sector, particularly public flagship universities. Indeed, even as greater numbers of students with demonstrated need enrolled in private colleges, the conventional wisdom on these campuses—and throughout higher education—was that public colleges and universities provided access for the masses through low tuition, whereas private colleges continued to serve a largely affluent population.

In this environment, forecasting revenue and enrollment was a relatively straightforward exercise in professional judgment. And although it would be misleading to suggest that colleges experienced no variation in application volume or yield, higher education was essentially a seller's market, rather than the buyer's market we know today, and there existed substantial market stability. Without a substantial public investment, variations in enrollment and revenue were linked more to economic conditions than to public funding and policy. Most colleges operated at a known capacity, had a historical sense of their retention rates and new student enrollments, and could project revenues and enrollments for budgeting and planning purposes in an unscientific but reliable manner. Revenue was simply gross tuition plus auxiliary income. The financial aid budget was established and predictable, part of the overall Education and General Expense budget. Attrition would occasionally depart from historical ranges, but in the main, the greatest difficulty lay in predicting residence hall utilization, a problem mainly created by liberalized college policies permitting greater numbers of students to live off campus.

Today, everything has changed. Private colleges and universities are forced to become acquainted with the new realities that challenge their pricing and finance structures. Among these are stagnating family income, minimal family savings, declining government support for grant programs, tuition levels that represent roughly twice the proportion of median household income as a decade ago, and a widening price gap with public sector counterparts. A brief exposition of these trends is useful to understand the ways in which private colleges and universities have chosen to predict and manage enrollments and revenues.

Since the late 1980s, family income for most population segments has stagnated and in some cases fallen in real terms. For private colleges and universities serving traditional age students, the economic anxiety affecting parents ages forty-five to fifty-four is apparent in the increased need demonstrated by most students, increased parental efforts to negotiate financial aid packages, the migration of students from affluent families to the public sector, and application trends favoring very selective institutions whose imprimatur is perceived as the greatest guarantor of future prosperity. Statewide studies performed since 1992 in Minnesota, Oregon, and Florida have documented not only this migration of affluent families to the public sector but also the minimal level of effort families of all income brackets make to save for college (Minnesota Private College Research Foundation, 1992; Florida Postsecondary Education Planning Commission, 1994; Oregon State System of Higher Education, 1995).

One of the common assumptions behind most higher education finance policy is that families bear the first responsibility to pay for college. Although poor families *cannot* save for college, these studies indicate that from one-third to one-half of the most affluent families *do not* save for college.

As federal and state grant aid have receded relative to inflation, replaced by increased federal loan eligibility, the dominant share of grant aid provided in private college financial aid packages comes from institutional sources, a trend documented by National Association of College and University Business Officers reports and many statewide and consortium studies. Indeed, at most private colleges, institutional grant aid exceeds state and federal sources combined. At the federal level, this trend is accelerated by the federalization of the needs analysis. This process removed the needs analysis function from its historical, independent, nonprofit providers—the College Scholarship Service (CSS), a unit of the College Board, and American College Testing—and eliminated the student fee. More important, the government liberalized the needs analysis formula itself, eliminating consideration of home equity, for example, and reducing the traditional needs analysis to a rationing device for federal aid. By defining more families as having need and as having greater need, the net result of federal policy has been to create a burgeoning unfunded mandate to meet student need. This situation is particularly vexing for private colleges and universities for several reasons, as most of their students demonstrated need under the old formula.

Some of these colleges continue to use the older, more rigorous methodology, which demands an additional effort from students. But their public competitors use federal methodology, which results in smaller family contributions, placing private institutions at a further disadvantage to their public sector competitors.

Moreover, many independent colleges historically have met the full need of students without "gapping" students, that is, failing to provide enough grant aid in the financial aid package to avoid surpassing the maximum Stafford loan. Increasingly, these colleges have been forced to slow, stop, or cannibalize academic investment to increase the financial aid budget to maintain enrollment.

Beyond shifting the burden for funding grant aid to students from government sources to the tuition and voluntary gift resources of the institution, these recent changes in the federal needs analysis, and resulting adjustments in college aid policies, have further complicated family financing of college, making the prediction of enrollment and revenue even harder. The three statewide studies have shown that for all but a small number of families, the federal needs analysis neither predicts nor defines family contribution.

As a result, the entire financial aid application process, an onerous endeavor to begin with, lacks public credibility. This credibility is further eroded as some colleges negotiate financial aid packages outside of the needs analysis or implement financial aid strategies that lack an explicit and intelligible philosophical foundation.

The main result of this combination of economic and policy circumstances has been to drive the price gap between public and private institutions to historical levels, both in published tuition rates and in the cost of college net of financial aid. In response to this price gap, increasing numbers and percentages of the most affluent families are enrolling their children in public sector institutions, especially flagship universities, taking advantages of state government subsidies that offset 50 to 80 percent of the cost of instruction. This trend is documented in national data and most demonstrably in each of the existing statewide family finance studies.

Beyond the public policy concerns about the equity and efficiency of higher-income families taking advantage of taxpayer tuition subsidies at public colleges, this oversupplied and increasingly price-competitive market means that private colleges and universities no longer can operate as relatively simple cash businesses. Though most college communities are loath to link their academic missions and public purposes to business comparisons, it simply is not useful to deny that higher education, like other goods and services in the economy, must "meet the market" and prove its value to those who pay the tab. In this way, college enrollment and revenue managers have more in common with marketing and inventory managers in the automobile, airline, and health care industries than they might care to admit. It is no surprise, in this context, to see that financial aid has become a price-discounting mechanism. Although colleges are now managing price strategically through financial aid, what they are unable to do with any flexibility is to manage capacity in the ways other industries do.

What are the specific results of these historical trends? Price again has become a barrier to a wide range of students attending private colleges. Because government grant aid is generally available only to the poorest private college students, the typical private college now enrolls a bifurcated student population—the very poor and the wealthy—with middle-income students taking up residence in the public sector.

Many private colleges are now locked in a vicious cycle of tuition discounting. They must provide more and more institutional grant aid in an attempt to maintain market share and the enrollment of middle-income families. To generate this aid, many colleges have pursued high-tuition strategies designed to generate the revenue necessary to support their programs, as they provide increased discounts in the form of grant aid. As higher tuition drives up family need, they must increase grant aid or lose enrollment and revenue. As their discount rates rise with the provision of more unfunded institutional aid, these colleges will inevitably reach a point at which any additional revenue generated by increased tuition will be committed to financial aid. At this point, when diminishing returns become negative returns, colleges will have to pursue alternative strategies to raise funds for needed academic investments.

Today, the average tuition discount rate for small, private liberal arts colleges is nearing 40 percent, but many are well past the 50 percent mark.

The operating objective for many private colleges now is not just to bring in an able freshman class or a class of a particular size, but rather to achieve enrollment that will produce a required level of net revenue. To do this, colleges now routinely differentiate grant aid in financial aid packages, rather than to simply address need equitably across the population of all admitted students, in an exercise that has become known as *financial aid leveraging*.

Financial aid leveraging implicitly recognizes that families will exhibit different levels of willingness-to-pay depending on their student's academic ability, the family's resources, and the reputation of the college. In a leveraging environment, institutional grant aid is awarded partly on the basis of need, partly on the basis of academic ability, and increasingly on subjective characteristics, such as leadership or citizenship, or on demographic grounds, such as state residency.

For example, a college or university may choose to award more generous grants to in-state students if they are located in states where state aid is available to students attending private colleges. Or, a college might provide scholarships for county residents if the school would like to enroll more local students but is priced too high for local incomes. Given the range of colleges, the competitive market conditions described above, and the very loose determination of need offered by the federal needs analysis, the assessment of need and ability-to-pay varies widely from school to school. In the days of need-based aid, when merit scholarships were rare, ability-to-pay and willingness-to-pay were assumed to be the same thing. Now they are two different but equally relevant variables in solving the matriculation equation.

Policy Crossroad

The financial aid community, in particular, laments the prevalence of differential financial aid awarding policies, but nearly all colleges, even those able to maintain purely need-based awarding, have had to recognize the penalty that rising financial aid commitments impose on their ability to fund academic investments. Thus, even those colleges whose aid is need driven may "gap" a segment of their freshman admits. In order to preserve their ability to meet the full need of admitted students, an increasing number of colleges make ability-to-pay a factor in late admission decisions.

From an economist's point of view, however, a market in which willingness-to-pay is the chief determinant in enrollment decisions benefits society as the ultimate source of equity by producing the most value, for the most people, at the lowest possible price. Because more and more families are not simply accepting a stated price, they exert greater power in the market, and colleges must be sensitive to the assessment these families make of the academic value offered by competing schools.

Houston, We Have a Problem

Given this environment, methodologies for predicting enrollment and revenue have become increasingly complex. Current predictive tools are statistically based, reliant on the ability to access and manipulate individual student-record data, and driven by the distribution of financial need among continuing and entering students as well as the net revenue contribution each will make.

For large, public institutions—particularly open-enrollment schools—being able to reliably predict revenue and enrollment has been a serious matter for some time. Dependent on taxpayer support, without the ability to manage class size through the admission process, these institutions must expand or contract programs based on the number of students who enroll year to year. With the majority of their revenues limited in the short-term by a set state appropriation and with tuition itself set far below the actual cost of instruction, these schools have been forced to develop an early warning system in order to manage their resources appropriately. In addition, for many of these schools, enrollment fluctuates dramatically with the health of the economy. Given their size, small percentage changes in student participation can cause major swings in costs and revenues.

To address these issues, public institutions have long used statistical models that consider such variables as tuition cost, high school graduation numbers, the health of the economy, and labor-market demand for various skills and occupations as they attempt to predict demand.

For private institutions—as for public ones—the complexity of predictive tools and models differs with the student population served (undergraduate versus graduate and professional), degree of selectivity, and the extent to which admission and financial aid notifications adhere to a single date or are presented on a rolling basis. For example, undergraduate liberal arts colleges with significant waiting lists experience a different and more manageable predictive challenge than do institutions that make admission decisions on a rolling basis and do not have the type of applicant pools to sustain a waiting list.

For highly selective liberal arts colleges, *predicting* enrollment and revenue is hard to separate from *managing* enrollment and revenue. Until recently, the challenge for these institutions was to predict the yield rate of admitted students. These colleges continue to manage this variable by establishing waiting lists of admitted students to provide replacements for those who decline offers of admission. Given the interlocking nature of the admitted student pool at many such colleges, managing yield to result in a class of a specific size, academic, or revenue profile can be a dicey exercise: one school's waiting list may be another school's regular admits.

More recently, as they recognized that the growth of their aid commitments was unsustainable, some highly selective liberal arts colleges have sought to manage enrollment yield through admission decisions and waiting lists and to manage revenue by linking admission policy with financial aid policy.

For example, Carleton College and Smith College have recommitted themselves to meeting the full need of admitted students. But they also have established a policy of need-sensitive admission for a fraction of their entering classes in order to assure that they will have the revenue needed to finance their financial aid commitments and maintain academic quality at the margin.

These colleges generally have not assigned a particular percentage of the class for need-sensitive consideration. To do so might needlessly erode the role and benefit of need-blind admission in building the strongest and most diverse class possible. Instead, they make this calculation on the run by assessing the amount of aid committed and likely to be accepted by matriculants and determining the amount of net revenue likely to result. At some point, need sensitivity is triggered to assure that budget targets are met—a process that places a greater premium on predictive models in the management of yield and budgets.

In general, the emphasis for these institutions is on managing to an enrollment objective that produces the desired revenue results, usually based on historical understandings of the composition and behavior of the entire admitted student population, not on developing an econometric statistical capacity to predict enrollment and revenue based on characteristics of particular student segments.

For other venerable but less selective colleges, budget predictions in the past were simply made in this conservative way, based on extrapolations of history. Although net revenues have become the defining objective of price and financial aid policies, many private college leaders who have a fixation on competition with other private colleges have failed to understand the effects of declining market share and the migration of students to the public sector. For this reason, they have set tuition relative to these private competitors and have concentrated on aid-focused competition with these colleges rather than attempting to reacquaint the larger market with the academic value they offer. Thus, as they consider next year's tuition increase, they often confront the reality that financial aid will effectively consume all of the revenue generated by the tuition hike.

Matrix Management

The new and inescapable reality in projecting enrollment and revenue for private colleges and universities is that one cannot be considered independent of the other. Participation in higher education has always been a function of price and value. But now, with from 50 percent to 90 percent of enrolled students receiving need- or merit-based financial aid, for most private colleges enrollment is now a function of net price, which differs from student to student based mainly on need and academic ability. Correspondingly, net revenue is a function of the ability and willingness of families to pay for a particular college based largely on its reputation. In order to predict enrollment and revenue, colleges have had to develop better understandings of the enrollment behavior of their continuing and entering students, assessing the role of many variables, especially academic characteristics, need, and grant aid.

As a by-product of efforts to maximize net revenue by leveraging financial aid or by reining in the financial aid budget, in recent years many private colleges have chosen to assess their admitted student pools by segmenting them based on levels of financial need and academic desirability. In doing so, colleges examine the number of students they are admitting and matriculating in each cell of the need-ability matrix and, based on the financial aid provided, calculate net revenue and attempt to manage and project enrollment and revenue. Here, financial aid leveraging means any strategic differentiation of institutional grant aid to affect the matriculation behavior of specific student groups to produce the desired results for net revenue or student profile (see Figure 4.1).

These matrices provide valuable information about the distribution of students and allow colleges to observe differing price response characteristics by student segment. To some extent, they allow colleges to see clearly for the first time the actual distribution of students that, taken together, produce such measures as the average Scholastic Assessment Test verbal score that is reported to college guide publications annually.

To the extent that a college can admit and then enroll the number of students who fall within particular cells that it needs, an enrollment management matrix can provide assurance that the college will meet its revenue and enrollment goals. Viewing a matriculation matrix over several years (which is essential to avoid charting a course based on an unusual year) allows a college to understand the stability of its admitted student population, economically and academically. It also can observe trends in matriculation rates relative to changes in grant aid.

Though matrices are essentially descriptive statistics—a picture of an entire entering cohort—in the hands of enrollment managers, they are potentially a more critical tool than even the most sophisticated econometric analysis. This is true for several reasons.

An enrollment management matrix in which admitted students are segmented by need, academic ability, and residency (in- and out-of-state residency) provides several important advantages that econometric models have difficulty providing. First, they describe the behavior of the entire population or large portions of it. This is important because for most private liberal arts colleges, the admitted student pool is too small to provide a robust basis for modeling behavior from one year to the next for smaller segments of the pool, such as likely orchestra members or African Americans.

Second, although the parametric matrix view does not provide a statistically tested basis for setting specific grant and matriculation targets for particular student segments, it does provide a framework within which a financial aid policy can be rationalized and its performance evaluated. Some practitioners of matrix-based financial aid analysis have suggested that a matrix segmentation that describes quality of financial aid package offered and resulting

Figure 4.1. Sample Matrices

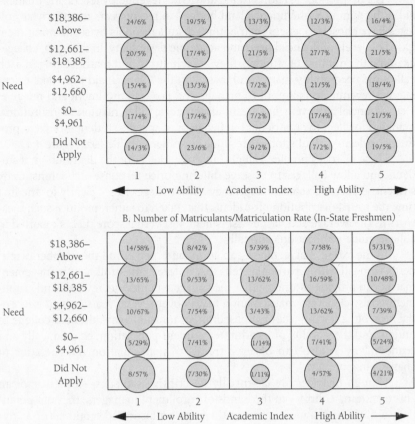

A. Number of Admits/Percentage of Total Admits (In-State Freshmen)

Need	1	2	3	4	5
$18,386–Above	24/6%	19/5%	13/3%	12/3%	16/4%
$12,661–$18,385	20/5%	17/4%	21/5%	27/7%	21/5%
$4,962–$12,660	15/4%	13/3%	7/2%	21/5%	18/4%
$0–$4,961	17/4%	17/4%	7/2%	17/4%	21/5%
Did Not Apply	14/3%	23/6%	9/2%	7/2%	19/5%

◄── Low Ability   Academic Index   High Ability ──►

B. Number of Matriculants/Matriculation Rate (In-State Freshmen)

Need	1	2	3	4	5
$18,386–Above	14/58%	8/42%	5/39%	7/58%	5/31%
$12,661–$18,385	13/65%	9/53%	13/62%	16/59%	10/48%
$4,962–$12,660	10/67%	7/54%	3/43%	13/62%	7/39%
$0–$4,961	5/29%	7/41%	1/14%	7/41%	5/24%
Did Not Apply	8/57%	7/30%	1/11%	4/57%	4/21%

◄── Low Ability   Academic Index   High Ability ──►

Overall matriculation rate: 45.5%; overall rate less NA: 48.1%

C. Average Total Grant Aid/Percentage Need Met (In-State Freshmen)

Need	1	2	3	4	5
$18,386–Above	$12114/58%	$11924/57%	$12268/61%	$13295/65%	$13877/66%
$12,661–$18,385	$9303/59%	$9141/60%	$10513/67%	$12662/77%	$12927/81%
$4,962–$12,660	$7629/80%	$7468/77%	$8366/73%	$9536/106%	$8666/97%
$0–$4,961	$1118/167%	$2632/294%	$2714/576%	$3976/624%	$4827/636%
Did Not Apply					

◄── Low Ability   Academic Index   High Ability ──►

matriculation rates amounts to a calculation of willingness-to-pay. This is not so. Only econometric modeling and simulation can provide this calculation. The difference between these two complementary tools is the difference between bracketing an aperture setting and using a light meter to take a picture in uncertain light.

But even when such a calculation is not available, the information it provides for setting targets for grant aid and matriculation cell by cell still must be evaluated with the help of the matrix analysis. And the matrix becomes essential for fitting this information into a coherent award policy and framework. The matrix is essential, too, for the management and evaluation of experiments a college may wish to take into the market to sound out particular student segments.

Because the relationship between grant aid and matriculation is not linear and differs for particular students, matrices cannot provide a statistically projectable estimate of price response—that is, they cannot tell you how much matriculation rates will change, if at all, given changes in awards levels. This is the role of econometric modeling.

Beyond its important role in setting targets and suggesting aid experiments within a matrix management framework, econometric modeling provides a predictive tool for matriculation rates in response to chosen grant aid targets.

The descriptive model provided by the matrix analysis and the projective model provided by econometric analysis complement each other. Each gives the other additional power. Whereas the limitations of the matrix are straightforward, the shortcomings of econometric analysis are more arcane and potentially dangerous. These limitations relate mainly to the small number of observations available and the need to cross-validate the matriculation significance of particular student characteristics over multiple years and data sets. In this process, researchers start with exploratory analysis of issues such as the multicolinearity of variables in order to understand which characteristics offer the best basis for model specification.

Observation shows that matriculation rates differ across student segments. In general, matriculation rates decline as academic ability increases: the stronger a student's academic qualifications, the greater his or her options. Matriculation rates will usually increase with the availability of grant aid. Correspondingly, as a rule, matriculation rates decline as need increases. But these differences are not uniform or consistent, either within a particular cohort or year to year. In fact, for many colleges, there is simply no linear correlation between the quality of financial aid package and matriculation (see Figure 4.2). For example, as indicated in Figure 4.2, there are low matriculation rates (less than 40 percent) at all levels of percentage of need met, whether it is 50 percent or almost 100 percent.

Because students with different characteristics demonstrate different elasticities of demand, some colleges are turning to more sophisticated statistical models to predict student behavior and thereby project enrollment and net revenue. Built on logistical (logit) regression techniques, these models explain matriculation as a function of multiple variables, such as grade point average, college

**Figure 4.2. Plot of Student Cohort Cells by Financial Aid
and Matriculation Rate**

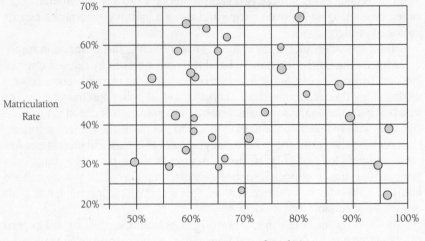

Percentage of Need Met

entrance test scores, class rank, the rigor of high school curricula, gender, status as an alumnus or alumna son or daughter, parental education attainment, state of residence, extracurricular participation, outside interests, and various indicators of family financial capability, including whether an aid application was made, the projected level of need, and the estimated family contribution.

As the regression analysis illuminates the role that each of these variables plays in matriculation, the college is in a better position to predict the behavior of students sharing a given characteristic. Indeed, with a sufficiently reliable model, colleges can identify the marginal effect on matriculation of, say, each additional $100 in grant aid. Understanding the effect of financial aid at the margin, a college can then calculate the net revenue available from a change in matriculation.

For this reason, multivariate modeling provides not only a predictive tool but also an important though limited addition to the matrix management tool. By running simulations of the effects of changes in grant aid in various student segments based on the outputs of the logit regressions, colleges may fine-tune their financial aid awarding strategies to achieve a combination of objectives relative to net revenue, enrollment, and student profile objectives, including diversity.

Analytic Framework

Although the analytic tools for econometric modeling are probably available at most colleges, it is helpful to establish a framework to guide the analytic exercise. For example:

Define enrollment capacity, by major or discipline, if possible.

Ascertain the sufficiency of the databases required to support the analysis.

Understand the state policy and economic environment.

Develop a historical understanding of the cumulative changes in state median household income compared with college tuition.

Achieve a historical, matrix-based understanding of admission, matriculation, financial aid packaging, and net revenue, by student segment.

Develop a multivariate analysis from tested variables that explains matriculation at a level at least 20 percentage points better than a random guess.

Simulate market response to incremental changes in grant aid, by segment.

Subject this analysis to rigorous interpretation and professional judgment based on historical understandings of student behavior across the entire population; set targets for aid and matriculation.

Rationalize a financial aid policy and award strategy to achieve college objectives and provide a coherent, legitimate treatment of all admitted students.

Establish targets for admission, matriculation, and net revenue.

Monitor, by drawing data into a matrix-based spreadsheet, the resulting composition of admits, matriculants, and net revenue on a weekly basis.

To a great extent, this kind of econometric analysis provides a backward-looking needs analysis, providing information that the current federal needs analysis no longer offers. It opens a window on willingness-to-pay that assesses the price-value calculation of students of various academic and economic backgrounds based on the past response of similar students to financial aid offers.

The Road Ahead

The kind of multivariate analysis and econometric modeling described above is the product of standard statistical tools but is controversial in its application to college pricing. To statisticians, logit regression is a tried-and-true arrow in the analytic quiver. To economists, the combination of private college tuition and financial aid policies is a classic example of price discrimination that occurs when the full price of desirable products is affordable only for a relative few, forcing providers to strive for an average net price and sales volume that will support provision of the product or service by utilizing discounts, financing options, and other pricing options.

This strategy is dangerous when the market deems a product less valuable than its price. And though the market may recognize that a college education pays dividends, increasingly families perceive that these dividends differ from college to college and are certainly not guaranteed. At the same time, higher education nationally suffers from overcapacity. There are many substitute products for most private colleges, including, for affluent students, the opportunity to capture sizable benefits through the tuition subsidies at public colleges and universities.

For all of these reasons, statistically based econometric models and simulations can provide private colleges with invaluable predictive and management tools. They also can be a source of poor and damaging judgments if colleges do not understand their limitations or do not utilize them within strong policy principles.

Although models and simulations are helpful, they are inherently mindless and heartless. They are fueled simply by the variables they consider, rendering simple situations needlessly complex or vice versa. The knowledge they provide will raise policy issues as well as questions of right and wrong. For example, if the application of these tools includes such variables as whether a student visited a campus, and analysis suggests that campus visits are statistically significant in explaining matriculation, then the college might perceive the opportunity to limit financial aid offers to students who have toured the campus. The model itself does not and cannot address the ethical, policy, or pragmatic issues this knowledge raises. So, knowledge about the factors that influence behavior, useful for predictive purposes, may be applied in ways that are damaging in the long run to the trust people have in the integrity of the college.

Because it is conventional wisdom in private college admissions operations that a campus visit is one of the better indicators of eventual matriculation, the question of whether aid offers should be differentiated on this basis has been discussed and resolved on most campuses. Most colleges see differentiation on this basis as unethical at worst and counterproductive at best, but the point remains that this kind of modeling demonstrates for colleges "the price of their principles," as one president has put it. Once they pursue the kind of knowledge models permit, colleges should be prepared to push interpretation of results to the policy level and to establish a strong set of principles from which to operate.

Conclusion

As private colleges and universities approach the turn of the century, they must once again operate independently of government support. To make the necessary adjustments in such areas as price, cost and financial structure, financial aid policy, and academic program delivery, colleges will have to understand the relatively new concept of enrollment management in increasingly sophisticated ways, bringing increasingly sophisticated tools to bear on the task.

In this process, colleges and universities increasingly will call on the institutional research office to provide predictive and management tools in the areas of marketing survey research, retention research, analysis of peer financial and market positions, and, of course, enrollment and net revenue modeling.

Clearly, such predictive tools are necessary in the current environment. Just as clearly, this environment creates distortions in market behavior that require greater sophistication than in the past if colleges are to achieve the required predictive capability. Like all data-based statistical tools, models of this kind are only as good as the information on which they are built and the institutional values that they support. In short, these tools are never more powerful than when interpreted and employed by ethical, intuitive professionals. More than ever, institutional researchers and enrollment managers will have to work collaboratively in teams that also include a college's data management personnel. Successful modeling cannot be a purely intellectual exercise, nor do most colleges today have the consistency in their databases required to support this kind of analysis. Building the necessary capacity will be a team endeavor.

References

Florida Postsecondary Education Planning Commission. *How Floridians Pay for College.* Technical Report of the Florida Family Funding Study. Tallahassee: Florida Postsecondary Education Planning Commission, July 1994.

Minnesota Private College Research Foundation. *Ways and Means: How Minnesota Families Pay for College.* St. Paul: Minnesota Private College Research Foundation, Nov. 1992.

Oregon State System of Higher Education. *Oregon Family Resource Study.* Eugene: Oregon State System of Higher Education, Aug. 1995.

JAMES H. DAY is president of Hardwick~Day, a consulting firm based in Minneapolis, which specializes in higher education–management issues. He was previously senior vice president of the Minnesota Private College Council and Research Foundation.

Enrollment forecasters have much to consider. A combination of quantitative and qualitative methods can sometimes be the best approach.

Methods and Techniques of Enrollment Forecasting

Paul T. Brinkman, Chuck McIntyre

Institutional researchers are often called on to conduct or assist with enrollment forecasts. Occasionally, personnel in institutional-planning offices, in state agencies, or in the marketing offices of continuing education divisions will be called on to produce such forecasts. Enrollment forecasts are fundamental elements of planning and budgeting at any higher education institution that depends on student enrollments or at any agency or organization that has responsibilities for supporting those institutions. Numerous institutional policy issues are related to enrollment forecasts—tuition policy, budget forecasting, faculty staffing, institutional closure or consolidation, and optimizing objectives related to the size and composition of enrollment (Weiler, 1987a).

There is no one right way to forecast enrollment. In this chapter, we discuss a variety of approaches and associated issues. We relate choices of method or technique to specific circumstances and situations in an effort to provide some guidance to readers in choosing their own approaches. We focus on forecasting institutional enrollments.

Factors Affecting Enrollment

No one factor determines enrollments at a college or university. For the economist, enrollment will be determined by the intersection of measured supply-and-demand curves. For the demographer, enrollments are related to numbers of people and where they are located. For the higher education administrator, enrollment is determined by the combined effects of many *manageable* and *unmanageable factors,* categories that are roughly, though not completely, equivalent to supply and demand. In addition, there is always the possibility that a

New Directions for Institutional Research, no. 93, Spring 1997 © Jossey-Bass Publishers given factor will differ in its impact by type of enrollment, for example, full-time versus part-time, traditional versus nontraditional, and so forth.

Unmanageable factors are those outside the institution that are typically associated with demand analysis, and just as typically—for college and university planning—associated with the investigation or scan of the external environment. Although innumerable trends and events are taking place "out there," the list of those affecting institutional enrollments is finite.

At the top of that list are *demographic factors* for the institution's service area, that is, the population's age structure, racial and ethnic composition, skill levels, and prior educational experience, as well as total inhabitants. Shifts in the location and existence of geographical constraints on transportation may also affect enrollment, especially for commuter schools.

A number of *economic factors* are relevant too, including the disposable incomes of potential students; unemployment rates; the general economic returns to college; and the demand for, and return to, training in specific areas. Economic cycles may also affect the institution's budget and, therefore, many of the factors that we include below under the manageable category. The impact may be more substantial on public than on private institutions because of the relationships between a state's economy and likely state revenues and appropriations. But, philanthropic support of private institutions, for example, also can be affected by economic conditions.

Social and *cultural factors* can be a good deal more ambiguous than economic factors in their impacts on enrollment. The change in the role of women in society has clearly increased enrollment substantially. The impact of other developments is less obvious. For instance, although entering students may, on average, be less prepared academically than prior generations, as measured by standard test scores, they also enter college with a greater facility in the use of information technology and with quite different learning styles. How this will affect enrollment through changing choices of programs, retention, and the like is not altogether clear, but probably there will be an impact.

Also relevant are the actions of *competitors,* that is, close substitutes, where students can pursue similar academic objectives. Decisions at these other institutions about their own manageable factors, such as tuition and fees, financial aid, admissions policies, changes in programs, and when and where they deliver services, may affect enrollment at one's own institution.

Finally, despite the efforts of many lobbyists, among those factors that institutions cannot manage is *public policy.* Policies that affect enrollments include legislatively set tuition and fees, admissions criteria, and degree requirements, along with other policies that alter the public's preferences for higher education generally or for specific institutions; for example, legislative pressure to make articulation easier between two-year and four-year colleges can lead to higher enrollments at the two-year colleges.

These unmanageable factors are at work, and ignoring them may well result in inaccurate forecasts. Even though one has little if any control over them, it is imperative that their impact on enrollment be assessed so that actions that can be managed are more likely to have the intended results.

Manageable factors include actions that are normally in the control of the institution. These factors often are discussed under the rubric of enrollment management. This topic has come into the spotlight during the past ten years, beginning in part with a proposed definition by Hossler and Kemerer (1986) in which the various functions or tools available to colleges and universities for managing enrollments were reviewed. Integration of the available management functions and tools was emphasized by Dolence (1989–1990), who more recently (1993) has expanded that notion to deal with the unmanageable factors in a process that he calls *strategic enrollment management.* Clagett (1992) provides a useful overview of the basic issues involved in enrollment management (see also McIntyre, 1995a).

Heading the list of manageable factors, though not included in all works on enrollment management, is the institution's *own pricing*—tuition (except for some public institutions), fees, residence hall costs, and financial aid. Also affecting enrollments are *marketing efforts, admissions policies and practices,* and *registration and course enrollment procedures.* Experience shows that these nonpricing activities, typically organized under student services, affect the preferences and capability of students to enroll. Unfortunately, empirical evidence that would quantify these influences is meager. Numerous studies address the *price-elasticity* of enrollment, but there is virtually nothing similar on the "marketing-elasticity" or "admissions-elasticity" of enrollment.

Also of importance in managing student enrollments are academic *probation and dismissal policies,* along with general efforts at student retention. The same is true for decisions by academic planners about *curriculum,* as the addition and deletion of programs and courses, length of programs, and location and scheduling of programs will affect the composition of enrollment as well as the total number of enrollees.

Perceptions of the *quality of instruction* will be crucial to determining enrollment at some institutions. Although perceptions may not be manageable directly, they can be influenced. Many factors will influence perceptions of quality. Can students get jobs after graduation? How is the institution rated? Although often quite subjective, ratings can have a substantial impact on perceived quality and therefore on enrollment. How attractive is what some observers call the *campus climate,* which includes student and other support services, such as counseling and placement, adequacy of facilities and the appearance of the campus, and the general academic and social environment in which students undergo their college experiences? In other words, virtually anything that might affect how students evaluate the investment and consumption benefits of attending an institution can influence their decisions to attend (or to stay enrolled).

Alternative Methodologies for Enrollment Forecasting

The objective of an enrollment forecast is a numerical estimate of a future enrollment level. Some approaches to arriving at that estimate rely on *quantitative* analyses, others rely on *qualitative* approaches.

Quantitative Methods.   Quantitative approaches to enrollment forecasting can be divided into two large families—*curve-fitting techniques (trend analyses)* and *causal (explanatory, structural, econometric) models.* The distinction between curve-fitting and causal models is very much the same as that used to distinguish, among stock analysts, the curve-fitters or "technicians" from the "fundamentalists," who concentrate on causal factors. Technicians believe that they can predict where a stock price is headed on the basis of patterns in the behavior of the price itself. By contrast, fundamentalists believe that company and industry characteristics are better guides to future stock prices. They look at demand for the company's products, its market share, the quality of its management, and so forth. (See Harris, 1996, for a discussion of these two approaches to analyzing stocks.)

Similarly, enrollment can be forecast entirely on the basis of prior enrollment patterns or on the basis of underlying fundamentals, such as the pool of potential students, the relative attractiveness of the institution in question, the enrollment slots supplied, the advent or demise of programs, the state of the economy, the demand for particular types and levels of skills, and so forth. The utility or appropriateness of a particular routine will depend on circumstances, such as the unit of analysis and the context and purpose of the forecast. Some combination of the two approaches is always an option. We discuss various specific approaches below and in the following section show how they have been used in enrollment forecasting.

Quantitative forecasting in the form of either curve-fitting techniques or causal models involves the analysis of historical data. At bottom, all such approaches are extrapolations of the past and are based on the assumption that patterns or relationships observed in prior time periods will continue into the future, at least to some degree.

Curve-fitting.   In curve-fitting, historical enrollment data are analyzed in an attempt to identify a pattern. This pattern is then extended to produce forecasts. Curve-fitting per se is oblivious to any future management decisions or environmental conditions that are different from those made in the past or to discontinuities of other kinds. Curve-fitting is most useful, therefore, when conditions can be expected to remain the same (for example, continuous growth) as they were during the relevant prior time periods. This approach is also useful as a means of portraying what would be the case if, in fact, patterns in the past were to continue.

The most rudimentary curve-fitting techniques are various forms of *simple* and *moving averages.* They will be more or less appropriate depending on the prior enrollment pattern. The *Box-Jenkins technique* is a complex form of moving average, as its alternative name, *autoregressive moving average,* indicates. It is used for short-term forecasts and is particularly appropriate for addressing trends and repetitive seasonal patterns. A commonly used method of averaging called *exponential smoothing* gives more weight to recent values. It is suitable for data that exhibit no apparent trends or seasonal patterns. Variations of this method, such as *Holt-Winters,* are suitable for dealing with trends and seasonal patterns. (See Hanke and Reitsch, 1992, for a discussion of these various techniques.)

Another approach to trend analysis is simply to regress the variable of interest, in this case enrollment, on time. Time, the independent variable, can be represented as a first-order *polynomial model* for a constant slope, a second-order polynomial for a slope that is headed up or down, and so forth. Or, one can estimate an *exponential model* in which the logarithm of enrollment is regressed on the logarithm of time. Statistical indicators, such as the standard error of estimate, and analysis of residuals can be useful in selecting the best functional form. (See Hanushek and Jackson, 1977, for helpful commentary on functional forms.)

Curve-fitting, or trend analysis, has the advantages of being easy to explain and not requiring much data compared to the typical causal model. It also has the virtue of incorporating, in effect, the combined impact of any influential variables that the analyst fails to specify when developing causal models. Curve-fitting can be applied either to enrollment or to enrollment ratios. Perhaps the most important disadvantage is that curve-fitting is not a useful tool for responding to "what if" questions about either the manageable or unmanageable influences on enrollment (Weiler, 1987a). Armstrong and Nunley (1981) examine some of the strengths and weaknesses of curve-fitting techniques for enrollment forecasting.

Causal Modeling.   In causal modeling of enrollment, attention shifts to the underlying factors that directly or indirectly influence enrollment levels. According to Wing (1974), there are several questions to answer when evaluating the appropriateness of causal models for enrollment forecasting: Are the model's independent factors really related to enrollments? Are the relationships between the independent factors and enrollments stable and predictable? Can the independent factors be forecast reliably? When these questions can be answered affirmatively, causal models are appropriate.

A common approach to causal modeling uses regression to estimate a longitudinal, multivariate, *enrollment demand model*. For example, historical, new, first-time enrollment—as the dependent variable—can be regressed on a set of historical, independent (explanatory, predictor) variables, such as the number of high school graduates, salaries for new college graduates, the unemployment rate, the institution's tuition, competitors' tuitions, student aid amounts, and the racial-ethnic composition of the population. The regression coefficients on the independent variables are estimates of the effects on enrollment (or an enrollment ratio, depending on model specification) of a one-unit change in the respective independent variables. These coefficients can then be used to forecast future enrollment levels—provided that estimates of future values of the independent variables are available or can be developed.

An enrollment ratio, such as the number of new freshmen enrolled over the number of high school graduates in the primary service area, is often the preferred form of the dependent variable. Typically, different models for new, first-time students; transfer students; and continuing students are estimated separately. Developing separate models for full-time, part-time, nontraditional, in-state, and out-of-state enrollments may also make sense depending on the institution.

The enrollment of graduate students usually is not addressed using models as described above. Demand models are designed to forecast enrollments that are determined by student demand. They are based on the assumption that the institution will admit all students who meet the institution's admission standards. This assumption would not hold for most graduate programs, for example, in which the number of students is determined as much by departments (that is, institutional supply) as by student demand. For the same reason, straightforward enrollment demand models do not make sense for institutions that restrict enrollment at the undergraduate level, although in both instances, one could legitimately develop demand models for applications to a program or institution rather than for actual enrollments. A confounding situation for the analyst occurs when an institution that offers unlimited enrollment de jure restricts enrollment de facto through such means as limiting the number of sections offered. This type of supply issue, which is often caused by budget considerations, can be represented within a causal model but not without addressing the problem of simultaneous equations bias (see McIntyre, 1995b; and especially Weiler, 1987b).

Causal modeling typically is complex. It can be a difficult path to follow without having, or having access to, experience in econometrics. For example, decisions need to be made regarding the form of the statistical model as well as the variables to include in it. Various statistics regarding model performance are generated by standard software programs, such as r-squared for overall model performance and the standard error of estimate for determining confidence intervals for predictions, the *Durbin-Watson statistic* for serial correlation in a *time-series* regression analysis, and t-scores for the statistical significance of individual independent variables. Considerable care must be taken in interpreting statistical indicators (see, for example, McCloskey and Ziliak, 1996). Interpretive skills are also needed in moving from statistical performance to analytical significance and on to implications for institutional policies or decisions.

Relevant Literature.   Systematic treatments of a range of quantitative enrollment-forecasting options are quite rare. Wing (1974) would qualify as one example; additional treatments reflecting new forecasting techniques would certainly be helpful. Articles focusing on a specific enrollment-forecasting technique are more plentiful as are articles reporting on specific influences on enrollments, such as the response of students to a change in the price of attendance.

Weiler (1987a) demonstrates how to design and use enrollment demand models, that is, models that incorporate the variables thought to influence the demand for enrollment systematically (see also Weiler, 1984). In a similar vein, Hoenack and Weiler (1979) develop a complex causal model for long-term enrollment forecasts. They focus on price and labor-market variables that influence demand for higher education and demonstrate procedures for calculating confidence intervals for an enrollment forecast. Salley (1979) argues that short-term forecasts often are more important for budgetary purposes than are long-term forecasts and shows how to distinguish the respective influence of cyclical, seasonal, and trend effects. Weiler (1980) too demonstrates a procedure for short-term forecasts, whereas Pope and Evans (1985), Chatman (1986), and Paulsen (1989) all show how to provide regular, updated monthly forecasts of the next term's enrollment. Pfitzner (1987) explains how to use a Box-Jenkins procedure in doing a short-term enrollment forecast.

Hopkins and Massy (1981) include a chapter on *student flow analysis,* an approach to forecasting the future enrollment of current students, in their review of modeling in higher education. They compare and contrast the virtues and data requirements of *grade progression–ratio methods* with *Markov chain models* and *cohort flow models.* Ewell (1987) also discusses Markov chains in the context of student flow models. Marshall and Oliver (1979) show how to estimate errors in student flow models. Rumpf, Coelen, and Creran (1987) demonstrate a student flow model that combines a *polynomial lag model* and a *goal programming model* and compare their results with other approaches to student flow analysis.

Thorpe (1990) discusses issues related to forecasting under conditions of discontinuity using an institution's transition from two-year college to four-year college. Kardonsky and Morishita (1990); Kraetsch (1979–1980); Clagett (1989); and Dickey, Asher, and Tweddale (1989) demonstrate the utility of disaggregating enrollment into behavioral subgroups before forecasting. Mixon (1992) and Mixon and Hsing (1994) employ economic theory and econometric techniques to forecast student migration and out-of-state enrollment. Frances (1989) and Jordan (1992) provide critiques of an overdependence on demographic projections as the basis for forecasting enrollments, especially at the state level. Strickland and others (1984) use both social and economic factors in estimating enrollment demand for a statewide system. Bingham (1993) demonstrates how enrollment forecasting might be done within the framework provided by marketing theory. Many studies have assessed the sensitivity of student demand to the price of attendance. Some twenty-five of these studies, through the mid 1980s, are reviewed in Leslie and Brinkman (1988). Some additional, more recent works in this area include Davis (1995), Tronvig and others (1993), Savoca (1990), and California Community Colleges (1993). On occasion, studies may focus on the use of estimated price-elasticities in setting pricing or student aid policies (for example, Hoenack and Weiler, 1975; McIntyre, 1982; Weiler, 1984; St. John, 1993).

Leslie and Brinkman (1988) also review numerous studies that address the effects of student aid on college attendance. More recently, Moore, Studenmund, and Slobko (1991) examine the effects of financial aid on enrollment at an individual, selective college. Parker and Summers (1993) examine the impact of tuition increases and financial aid on enrollments at liberal arts colleges.

Alexander and Frey (1984) and McLain, Vance, and Wood (1984) discuss enrollment forecasts and admissions yield, respectively, in the context of master of business administration programs. Weiler (1987b) demonstrates an econometric technique for dealing with supply-constrained graduate enrollments at public universities.

Miller and McGill (1984) examine the influence of economic expansion on enrollment, as does Salley (1979). Kroncke and Ressler (1993) show how fluctuations in the unemployment rate, which changes the price ratio of public to private higher education, have enrollment ramifications for the two sectors.

Finally, basic texts on forecasting per se are available. For example, Hanke and Reitsch (1992) and Jarrett (1991) provide quite useful texts that show how a wide range of statistical techniques can be used to develop forecasts. O'Donovan (1983) is another example of this genre, but with a narrower focus—the Box-Jenkins approach.

Qualitative Methods.   Qualitative enrollment forecasting often involves consulting with a group of experts, securing their individual opinions, and trying to arrive at a consensus. This technique can range in rigor from a casual discussion to a formal, several-round *Delphi process*. Between these extremes are techniques such as the *triad, nominal group,* and *charrette techniques.* In all cases, the forecaster seeks to derive a group forecast that is more reliable than would be possible from one individual or from many individuals working in isolation without the benefit and feedback from others' thinking. Though some would argue that the qualitative approach is better for long-term forecasts (O'Donovan, 1983), surveys do not indicate such a preference among professional forecasters in the business sector (Jain, 1987). A more widely endorsed argument for resorting to qualitative methods is a lack of useful historical quantitative data.

These qualitative exercises may involve thinking about the unmanageable factors, that is, the future values of trends and events external to the institution that are addressed by environmental scanning and futures research. An enrollment forecaster may want to combine the above group techniques with such analytical *futures-research techniques* as *probability impact, impact network, cross impact, policy impact, scenario-writing, issues management,* and others in order to complete the forecasting task (see, for example, McIntyre, 1991; Morrison, Renfro, and Boucher, 1984).

Qualitative approaches may also focus on the manageable factors that may reflect changes in supply—not just the number of courses but time and location as well—or changes in policies that could impact admission or retention. As a rule, policy changes are difficult to address in a quantitative-only approach because they typically involve a discontinuity of sorts, that is, a break with the past that may invalidate methods based inherently on the appropriateness of extrapolating the past into the future.

The literature on qualitative enrollment-forecasting methods is relatively meager. However, basic texts on forecasting, such as Hanke and Reitsch (1992) and Jarrett (1991), which were mentioned earlier, do include sections on qualitative methods. Jain (1987) is an example of a text devoted entirely to the topic that may also be referred to as *judgmental forecasting.*

Combined Approaches. In practice, many higher education institutions use a combination of quantitative and qualitative approaches. The former is more likely to involve a formal methodology and the latter an informal one in which, at a minimum, forecasts have to pass a face-validity test—that is, whether they seem plausible.

One way of combining a quantitative with a more formal qualitative approach is to graph the pattern(s) of unexplained residuals, or errors, resulting from a quantitative-forecasting model applied to prior enrollments and then convene a group of experienced institutional experts or market experts such as high school counselors to identify the possible causes for such error, causes which may well be subject only to qualitative specification. This process can often shed light on particular policies or practices whose existence or nonexistence may have a major impact on enrollment.

Weissman (1994) provides an example of a hybrid approach in which regression routines are used to develop statistical relationships between service-area populations and enrollments (course registrations) in disciplines. The resulting forecasts, based on population projections for the service area, are then adjusted by academic administrators in the disciplines, as they consider various factors, including supply (for example, number of sections to be offered), which might affect enrollment. The process requires much communication and consensus building among several college areas. Armstrong and Nunley (1981) discuss how they used a combination of quantitative-forecasting techniques along with a qualitative, highly consultative approach.

Although the transition rates or transition probabilities used in student flow models are quantitative in nature, such models provide a convenient structure for analyzing the effect of policies—for example, the adoption of a *rising junior examination*—on those rates or probabilities. The incorporation of the policy change dimension will likely be done in a qualitative way, given the likely absence of relevant historical data on which to draw.

A word of warning is in order, however. When suitable historical data are available to support quantitative methods, modifying the results of such analyses with a judgmental component tends to reduce the accuracy of the forecasts and add to their costs (Makridakis, 1986). Accordingly, such modifications must be done with care, perhaps only when there is an obvious reason to do so, such as a policy shift or a major discontinuity in the environment. The analyst needs to guard against sources of judgmental bias, such as political considerations or just plain wishful thinking.

Application and Implementation Issues for the Analyst

Many options are available for enrollment forecasting. Following is a list of things to consider when selecting a forecasting approach.

What is the purpose of the forecast? Will it be used for policy analysis, particularly for evaluating policies that might affect enrollment? If the latter is the case, then the forecast ought to be sensitive to policy options—that is, alternative policies should lead to different forecasts. Some sort of causal model or qualitative approach would likely be required. Causal models require more data than curve-fitting models. Can such data be found or developed? Is there sufficient understanding, if not a theory, on which to build a causal model? Can enrollment or enrollment rates be linked to something in the environment or in the institution? A curve-fitting approach might suffice if all that is needed is an extrapolation from the past. A good strategy can be to use both approaches and compare the results.

Are there target-population subgroups that may behave differently, or will a single forecast suffice? Groupings such as resident versus nonresident, male versus female, traditional age versus nontraditional age (or other background), first-time versus transfer, entering versus continuing, vocational versus academic, and various racial-ethnic categories are among those worth considering.

What is the minimum acceptable level of forecasting accuracy? Typically, the factors that determine the suitable level of accuracy are the importance of the management decision being made, which often reflects the financial risks involved, and the role of the forecast in affecting that decision. Although the effort expended is likely to make a difference, accuracy will ultimately depend on the validity and reliability of historical data, the accuracy of relevant assumptions, the appropriateness of the forecasting technique, and the inherent stability in the type of enrollment being forecast. It may be prudent to develop a forecast interval rather than depend on a point estimate. An interval could take the form of two forecasts—one reflecting the result of optimistic assumptions and the other based on pessimistic assumptions regarding, for example, participation rates or the pool of potential students. Or the bounds of the interval could simply be the results of forecasts derived from different techniques, or they could be boundaries of a confidence interval derived from an econometric model.

The unit of analysis will affect how one approaches an enrollment forecast. For example, marketing issues might be paramount when forecasting enrollment for a proposed new instructional site but not particularly important when forecasting enrollment for an entire system of institutions. Social and demographic issues will perhaps be of greater importance for state-level forecasts than for institutional-level forecasts. Institutional management strategies will figure more importantly in the latter. In particular, issues of model specification and interpretation will depend on whether the analyst must take into account factors that influence students to choose a specific institution when close substitutes are available (Weiler, 1987a). Some issues, such as an *inter-institutional flow model* for transfer students, can best be addressed at the state or system level.

Is the enrolling entity, whether it be a program, institution, or system, in a position to accept whatever demand arises, or are there explicit or hidden supply constraints (within a reasonable range of possible demand)? Many institutions that erect few formal barriers to admission constrain enrollment by other means; limiting the number of sections offered in conjunction with class size limitations is a prime example.

Who should be consulted regarding the forecast because of actions they may take that could affect enrollment, because they may have special insight about enrollment, or because they will use the forecast and will have to find it credible? Are there enrollment management activities to be taken into account?

How difficult is it to understand a proposed forecasting approach? Policymakers may not have confidence in a forecast if they do not understand its conceptual basis or accept its assumptions.

How much will it cost to develop and run the forecasting model? The costs of data gathering, model development, and model management will vary considerably depending on the approach. For example, simple exponential smoothing would be much less costly than a multivariate causal model.

What is the appropriate time frame for the forecast: Short-term, long-term, or something in between? Next year's operating revenues, strategic plans, and capital plans are likely to require increasingly long time frames.

Conclusion

As noted at the start, there is no one right way to forecast enrollment. In many instances, it will likely be prudent to use a combination of approaches. Clearly, the analyst should get everything possible from the quantitative historical record. But forecasts based on that record need to be weighed against possible changes in supply, in relevant policies, and in the environment. Methods need to be selected that make sense with respect to the questions being addressed, the policies and decisions at stake, the time and talent required, and a host of other dimensions discussed above. Given that computer resources are now ubiquitous and data are increasingly accessible, the temptation is to start quickly, but enrollment forecasting is one activity for which careful preparation will likely be worth the effort.

References

Alexander, E. R., and Frey, D. E. "An Econometric Estimate of the Demand for MBA Enrollment." *Economics of Education Review 1984, 3,* 97–104.

Armstrong, D. F., and Nunley, C. W. "Enrollment Projection Within a Decision-Making Framework." *Journal of Higher Education,* 1981, *52* (3), 295–309.

Bingham, B., Jr. "Marketing the Institution of Higher Learning: A Research Analysis Enrollment Model." *Journal of Marketing for Higher Education,* 1993, *4* (1/2), 59–72.

California Community Colleges. *Study of Fee Impact: Phase 2, 1993.* Sacramento, Calif.: Office of the Chancellor, May 1993. (ED 355 998)

Chatman, S. P. "Short-Term Forecasts of the Number and Scholastic Ability of Enrolling Freshmen by Academic Divisions." *Research in Higher Education,* 1986, *25* (1), 68–81.

Clagett, C. *Credit Headcount Forecast for Fall 1989–90: Component Yield Method Projections. Planning Brief PB90–3.* Largo, Md.: Prince Georges Community College, 1989. (ED 325 162)

Clagett, C. "Enrollment Management." In M. A. Whiteley, J. D. Porter, and R. H. Fenske (eds.), *The Primer for Institutional Research*. Tallahassee, Fla.: Association for Institutional Research, 1992.

Davis, G. W. "Tuition and Fee Increases and Community College Enrollments." *Community College Journal of Research and Practice*, 1995, *19* (1), 13–21.

Dickey, A. K., Asher, E. J., Jr., and Tweddale, R. B. "Projecting Headcount and Credit Hour Enrollment by Age Group, Gender, and Degree Level." *Research in Higher Education*, 1989, *30* (1), 1–19.

Dolence, M. G. "Evaluation Criteria for an Enrollment Management Program." *Planning for Higher Education*, 1989–90, *18* (1), 1–14.

Dolence, M. G. *Strategic Enrollment Management: A Primer for Campus Administrators*. Washington, D.C.: American Association of Collegiate Registrars and Admissions Officers, 1993.

Ewell, P. T. "Principles of Longitudinal Enrollment Analysis: Conducting Retention and Student Flow Studies." In J. A. Muffo and G. W. McLaughlin (eds.), *A Primer on Institutional Research*. Tallahassee, Fla.: Association for Institutional Research, 1987.

Frances, C. "Uses and Misuses of Demographic Projections: Lessons for the 1990s." In A. Levine and Associates (eds.), *Shaping Higher Education's Future: Demographic Realities and Opportunities, 1990–2000*. San Francisco: Jossey-Bass, 1989.

Hanke, J. E., and Reitsch, A. G. *Business Forecasting*. (4th ed.) Needham Heights, Mass.: Allyn & Bacon, 1992.

Hanushek, E. A., and Jackson, J. E. *Statistical Methods for Social Scientists*. Orlando, Fla.: Academic Press, 1977.

Harris, S. J. *Trading 101: How to Trade Like a Pro*. New York: Wiley, 1996.

Hoenack, S. A., and Weiler, W. C. "Cost-Related Tuition Policies and University Enrollments." *Journal of Human Resources*, 1975, *10*, 332–360.

Hoenack, S. A., and Weiler, W. C. "The Demand for Higher Education and Institutional Enrollment Forecasting." *Economic Inquiry*, 1979, *17*, 89–113.

Hopkins, D., and Massy, W. F. *Planning Models for Colleges and Universities*. Stanford, Calif.: Stanford University, 1981.

Hossler, D., and Kemerer, F. "Enrollment Management and Its Context." In D. Hossler (ed.), *Managing College Enrollments*. New Directions for Higher Education, no. 53. San Francisco: Jossey-Bass, 1986.

Jain, C. L. (ed.). *A Managerial Guide to Judgmental Forecasting*. Flushing, N.Y.: Graceway, 1987.

Jarrett, J. *Business Forecasting Methods*. (2nd ed.) Oxford, England: Basil Blackwell, 1991.

Jordan, S. M. "Enrollment Demand in Arizona: Policy Choices and Social Consequences." In J. I. Gill and L. Saunders (eds.), *Developing Effective Policy Analysis in Higher Education*. New Directions for Institutional Research, no. 76. San Francisco: Jossey Bass, 1992.

Kardonsky, S., and Morishita, L. "Cohort Stripping: An Enrollment Projection Technique." Paper presented at the meeting of the Society for College and University Planning, Atlanta, July 1990.

Kraetsch, G. A. "Methodology and Limitations of Ohio Enrollment Projections." *Association for Institutional Research Professional File*, no. 4, Winter 1979–80.

Kroncke, C. O., Jr., and Ressler, R. W. "The Alchian-Allen Effect in Higher Education: Public Versus Private Enrollment." *Economics of Education Review*, 1993, *12* (4), 345–349.

Leslie, L. L., and Brinkman, P. T. *The Economic Value of Higher Education*. Old Tappan, N.J.: Macmillan, 1988.

McCloskey, D., and Ziliak, S. "The Standard Error of Regressions." *Journal of Economic Literature*, 1996, *34* (1), 97–114.

McIntyre, C. "Price-Elasticity of Demand for Two-Year College Enrollment." Paper presented at the annual conference of the Western Economic Association, Los Angeles, June 1982.

McIntyre, C. "Using Futures Research for Planning and Decisionmaking." Preconference seminar presented at the annual forum of the Society for College and University Planning, Seattle, Wash., July 1991.

McIntyre, C. "Enrollment Forecasting to Support Proactive Issues Management." Paper presented at the annual forum of the Society for College and University Planning, San Antonio, Tex., July 1995a.

McIntyre, C. *Study of Tuition and Fees.* Report prepared under contract to Maricopa County Community College District, Sacramento, Calif., 1995b.

McLain, D., Vance, B., and Wood, E. "Understanding and Predicting the Yield in the MBA Admission Process." *Research in Higher Education,* 1984, *20,* 55–76.

Makridakis, S. "The Art and Science of Forecasting." *International Journal of Forecasting,* 1986, *2,* 15–39.

Marshall, K. T., and Oliver, R. M. "Estimating Errors in Student Enrollment Forecasting." *Research in Higher Education,* 1979, *11* (3), 195–205.

Miller, J. C., and McGill, P. A. "Forecasting Student Enrollment." *Community and Junior College Journal,* 1984, 31–33.

Mixon, F. G., Jr. "Factors Affecting Student Migration Across States." *International Journal of Manpower,* 1992, *13* (1), 25–32.

Mixon, F. G., Jr., and Hsing, Y. "The Determinants of Out-of-State Enrollments in Higher Education: A Tobit Analysis." *Economics of Education Review,* 1994, *13* (4), 329–335.

Moore, R. I., Studenmund, A. H., and Slobko, T. "The Effect of the Financial Aid Package on the Choice of a Selective College." *Economics of Education Review,* 1991, *10* (4), 311–321.

Morrison, J., Renfro, W., and Boucher, W. *Futures Research and the Strategic Planning Process: Implications for Higher Education.* ASHE-ERIC Higher Education Report, no. 9. Washington, D.C.: Association for Study of Higher Education, 1984.

O'Donovan, T. M. *Short Term Forecasting: An Introduction to the Box-Jenkins Approach.* New York: Wiley, 1983.

Parker, J., and Summers, J. "Tuition and Enrollment Yield at Selective Liberal Arts Colleges." *Economics of Education Review,* 1993, *12* (4), 311–324.

Paulsen, M. B. "A Practical Model for Forecasting New Freshmen Enrollment During the Application Period." *College and University,* 1989, *64* (4), 379–391.

Pfitzner, C. B. "A Short-Term Forecasting Procedure for Institution Enrollments." *Community/Junior College Quarterly of Research and Practice,* 1987, *11* (3), 142–152.

Pope, J. A., and Evans, J. P. "A Forecasting Model for College Admissions." *College and University,* 1985, *60* (2), 113–131.

Rumpf, D. L., Coelen, S. P., and Creran, F. J. "Estimating Post-Secondary Student Flow with Limited Data." *Research in Higher Education,* 1987, *27* (1), 39–50.

St. John, E. "Untangling the Web: Using Price Response Measures in Higher Education." *Journal of Higher Education,* 1993, *64* (6), 676–695.

Salley, C. D. "Short-Term Enrollment Forecasting for Accurate Budget Planning." *Journal of Higher Education,* 1979, *50* (3), 323–333.

Savoca, E. "Another Look at the Demand for Higher Education: Measuring the Price Sensitivity of the Decision to Apply to College." *Economics of Education Review,* 1990, *9* (2), 123–134.

Strickland, D. C., and others. "Effects of Social and Economic Factors on Four-Year Higher Education Enrollments in Virginia." *Research in Higher Education,* 1984, *20* (1), 35–53.

Thorpe, S. W. "Forecasting Enrollment in a Period of Institutional Transition." Paper presented at the annual Northeastern Association for Institutional Research Conference, Albany, N.Y., Oct. 21–23, 1990. (ED 328 134)

Tronvig, J. A., and others. *The Impact of the Differential Enrollment Fee on Chaffey College Baccalaureate Students.* Rancho Cucamonga, Calif.: Chaffey College, 1993. (ED 361 021)

Weiler, W. C. "A Model for Short-Term Institutional Enrollment Forecasting." *Journal of Higher Education,* 1980, *50* (3), 314–327.

Weiler, W. C. "Using Enrollment Demand Models in Institutional Pricing Decisions." In L. L. Litten (ed.), *Issues in Pricing Undergraduate Education.* New Directions for Institutional Research, no. 42. San Francisco: Jossey-Bass, 1984.

Weiler, W. C. "Enrollment Demand Models and Their Policy Uses in Institutional Decision Making." In J. C. Smart (ed.), *Higher Education: Handbook of Theory and Research,* vol. 3. New York: Agathon Press, 1987a.

Weiler, W. C. "Enrollment Demand with Constrained Supply in a Higher Education Institution." *Research in Higher Education,* 1987b, 27 (1), 51–61.

Weissman, J. "Enrollment Projections: Combining Statistics and Gut Feelings." *Journal of Applied Research in the Community College,* 1994, 1 (2), 143–152.

Wing, P. *Higher Education Enrollment Forecasting: A Manual for State-Level Agencies.* Boulder, Colo.: National Center for Higher Education Management Systems, 1974.

PAUL T. BRINKMAN *is director of planning and policy studies at the University of Utah–Salt Lake City.*

CHUCK MCINTYRE *is director of research in the policy analysis and development division of the state chancellor's office of California Community Colleges, Sacramento.*

Although revenue forecasting is an integral part of the budgeting
process for all institutions of higher education, institutions vary
in their approaches to this critical task. Colleges and universities
determine their forecasting methods and techniques based on the
institution's reliance on various sources of revenue and the internal
and external environment that has impact on each of those sources.

Methods and Techniques of Revenue Forecasting

J. Kent Caruthers, Cathi L. Wentworth

Classic budgeting theory calls first for the determination of funds to be available, that is, a revenue forecast, and then for the development of a spending plan that typically will require no more funds than those expected to be available. The practice of planned expenditures not exceeding budgeted revenue during an individual fiscal year is especially ingrained in the public sector. The laws of most states require public institutions to submit budget requests and subsequently operate under balanced budgets. Unlike the extensive literature on how to develop spending plans using peer institution or benchmark data, formula guidelines, or internal reallocation techniques, revenue forecasting is a relatively underdeveloped (or at least underdocumented) aspect of budgeting practice for colleges and universities.

Beyond the legal or policy-based requirement of needing to know how much funding will be available before deciding where and how to spend the money, accurate revenue projections are now of even greater importance due to the current economic environment. Most institutions are currently functioning in a period of tight finances in which few colleges have the luxury of being able to hold back a significant level of operating reserves in their annual budgets as protection against overly optimistic projections. Not only do they find it difficult to budget a reserve in their current allocations, but most institutions have relatively low levels of accumulated financial surpluses from prior

We wish to express appreciation to officials at the following institutions for sharing their experiences and practices: Appalachian State University, Azusa Pacific University, Florida State University, George Mason University, Pensacola Junior College, Point Loma Nazarene College, and Tallahassee Community College.

years that can be used to offset the impact of inaccurate revenue projections. In addition, with an ever increasing proportion of campus budgets being committed to personnel costs (particularly tenured faculty positions), institutions face significant difficulties in implementing midyear expenditure reductions when their revenue projections fail to materialize.

The purpose of this chapter is to identify and analyze several factors that college and university budget planners should consider in the development of revenue forecasts. The chapter also includes a discussion of how different types of institutions of higher education prepare forecasts for each major source of revenue.

Analysis of Revenue by Source

Institutions of higher education typically have multiple revenue sources, including student tuition and fees, gifts and grants, auxiliary enterprises, and government appropriations. Many of these revenue streams are interdependent. For example, both tuition and state appropriations may be dependent on the number of students, and the methods used to forecast revenue for one of the sources might carry over into the methods used to develop projections for the next source. Other revenue sources are largely unrelated to one another and, thus, would appear to require unique revenue projection techniques.

As shown in Table 6.1, the relative importance of the different types of revenue vary by the instructional mission and the control of the institution (public versus private).

For all U.S. colleges and universities in 1993–94, approximately 30.4 percent of the total revenues came from student tuition and fees. Private institutions, however, are much more dependent on this source (which accounts for 46.7 percent of total revenues in this sector). In recent years, public institutions have become increasingly dependent on revenue from student tuition and fees. In 1985–86, tuition and fees accounted for 15.7 percent of revenues as compared with 20.7 percent in 1993–94, as state governmental appropriations for public higher education declined from 46.6 percent in 1985–86 to 37.3 percent in 1993–94. Accordingly, student charges for tuition and fees have become a much more critical component of the revenue projection methodology for public colleges and universities.

Government appropriations (usually state appropriations) represent a major source of revenue for public institutions, especially two-year institutions. Public institutions, and to a lesser degree private institutions in states with tuition equalization grant programs, need to devote special efforts in their revenue-forecasting process toward monitoring the development of state and local budgets.

As of the fiscal year 1993–94, private institutions were more dependent on the federal government (16.1 percent of total revenue) than were public institutions (12.4 percent of total revenue), whereas public colleges and universities relied more on state and local governments (44.8 percent of total revenue) than did private colleges (3.1 percent of total revenue).

Table 6.1. Sources of Revenue for Colleges and Universities, 1993–94 (percentage)

	All Institutions	All Public	Public 4-Year	Public 2-Year	All Private
Tuition and Fees	30.4	20.7	20.4	21.6	46.7
Federal Government					
Appropriations	1.2	1.8	2.1	0.5	0.4
Unrestricted grants and contracts	2.0	1.7	2.0	0.3	2.4
Restricted grants and contracts	8.5	8.7	9.8	4.5	8.0
Independent operations	2.1	0.2	0.2	0.1	5.3
Subtotal	13.8	12.4	14.1	5.4	16.1
State Governments					
Appropriations	23.6	37.3	37.0	38.3	0.4
Unrestricted grants and contracts	0.2	0.3	0.2	0.4	0.2
Restricted grants and contracts	2.3	2.7	2.4	3.9	1.7
Subtotal	26.2	40.3	39.6	42.7	2.3
Local Governments					
Appropriations	2.5	4.0	0.3	18.9	0.0
Unrestricted grants and contracts	0.1	0.1	0.1	0.2	0.1
Restricted grants and contracts	0.5	0.4	0.4	0.4	0.7
Subtotal	3.1	4.5	0.7	19.4	0.8
Private Gifts, Grants and Contracts					
Unrestricted	2.1	0.7	0.8	0.2	4.5
Restricted	4.2	3.8	4.6	0.7	5.0
Subtotal	6.4	4.5	5.4	0.9	9.5
Endowment					
Unrestricted	1.0	0.3	0.3	0.1	2.2
Restricted	1.3	0.4	0.5	0.0	2.9
Subtotal	2.3	0.6	0.8	0.1	5.1
Sales and Services					
Educational activities	3.3	3.3	4.0	0.7	3.3
Auxilary enterprises	10.9	10.7	11.9	6.3	11.3
Subtotal	14.2	14.0	15.8	7.0	14.6
Other Sources	3.7	3.0	3.1	2.9	4.8
Total	100.0	100.0	100.0	100.0	100.0

Note: Excludes revenue from hospitals. Totals may not sum to 100 percent due to rounding.

Source: U.S. Department of Education, 1995.

Institutions with large endowments are most likely to be concerned with the revenue from private giving. Similarly, revenue from contracts and grants has the greatest impact on universities whose mission is largely research. An institution's focus on particular types of revenue is likely to shift over time, however, according to adjustments in the nation's economy and governmental appropriation policies and priorities. For example, overall revenues from tuition and fees have increased by 21 percent in less than a decade, whereas revenues from the federal government have decreased 29 percent, accompanied by a 23 percent decrease in state appropriations for higher education. Therefore, it is important that the leaders of colleges and universities work to diversify their sources of revenue in order to increase their options when facing a revenue shortfall (Brinkman, 1990).

Major Categories of Variables in a Revenue Projection Model

On one hand, the task of forecasting revenue seems simple enough. One only needs to multiply the projected enrollment levels by the scheduled tuition rates to derive a forecast of tuition revenue. Similarly, the forecast of governmental appropriations might be determined by multiplying the institution's historical share of the state budget by the statewide revenue projection.

On the other hand, and as the examples cited illustrate, revenue projections are frequently based on numbers that are themselves projections. This means that the successful forecaster of institutional revenues must either know where to find valid projections of each variable or become an expert in these areas. This may be the reason some people believe that revenue projections are "best left to economists" (Meisinger, 1994, p. 12). We contend, however, that this does not need to be the case. Experienced budget managers are capable of making accurate projections by using their own resources and collaborating with others on and off campus.

In particular, the higher education budget planner must consider at least three types of variables in developing revenue estimates—enrollment, economic conditions, and social conditions.

Links Between Enrollment and Revenue. For the vast majority of colleges and universities, the number of students to be enrolled is probably the most important variable in developing revenue projections as several of the major sources of revenue are enrollment driven. The most obvious link between enrollment and revenue levels, of course, is student tuition and fees. A shortfall in the number of students enrolled almost certainly leads to a corresponding shortfall in available tuition revenues to operate the institution. For public institutions in states with enrollment-driven funding formulas, the number of students is also a key factor in determining state appropriations. Further, charges to students are the major component of another source of revenue, auxiliary enterprises.

Despite the direct impact that the number of students enrolled can have on available revenues, the link between enrollment and budget levels is not unidirectional. Certain revenue-planning decisions can significantly affect the number of students who choose to enroll. For instance, decisions about tuition levels may affect decisions by students about where (or even whether) to enroll. The impact on enrollment levels of revenue decisions about tuition rates, of course, can further be affected by expenditure budget decisions about the amount of financial aid to be made available.

Links Between Economic Conditions and Revenue.   A second major external variable to consider in college and university revenue projections is the economy. Economic conditions can have a direct influence on revenues from governmental appropriations, governmental grants and contracts, and private giving. Economic conditions are also likely to have an indirect impact on tuition revenues through their influence on the enrollment decisions of individual students.

When state and local governments begin their budget development processes, one of the first steps is the revenue forecast. Similar to colleges and universities, the revenues for state and local governments come from a variety of sources. Separate revenue projection models are typically used for each source, for example, the sales tax, the income tax, the fuels tax, the license fees, and so forth. Projections for the several types of tax revenue are often based on historical trends, augmented by national economic forecasts. Likewise, the revenue projected from user fees is based on recent experience and information about scheduled rate changes.

The revenue forecasts in many states are updated periodically during the budget development cycle, based on the most recent experience in actual collections. The campus-based budget planner can anticipate future levels of governmental appropriations by monitoring economic conditions in his or her jurisdiction. Most states have a formal process for monitoring collections, which involves executive and legislative economic forecasting experts who meet regularly to review collections and, as necessary, to revise projections. Monitoring can be important both during the budget development process before the appropriations bill is enacted as well as after the fiscal year has begun and revenue shortfalls threaten a midyear reduction in appropriations.

Institutions of higher education, particularly community colleges, often feel the impact of the economy as they determine trends in their local workforces, thereby influencing decisions about new instructional program development as the institutions strive to meet the ever changing needs of their communities. The development of new programs often accompanies the discontinuance of current programs that are no longer in great demand. These programmatic changes may result in a change in revenue through tuition, enrollment, and state or local appropriations, depending on the nature and purpose of the new program. Campus budget planners may find it useful to communicate regularly with the program-planning staff to remain abreast of any new program development and trends in the job market of the local community.

Economic conditions also influence the level of private giving for institutions of higher education. During times of sustained economic growth, potential donors are likely to have either more confidence in their employment security and future earnings or a strong tax incentive to offset investment income with charitable contributions. On the other hand, potential donors are more prone to conserve their resources in more uncertain economic times (Ryan, 1994). Campus budget planners may need to review their own institution's experience with private giving during different phases of an economic cycle to determine whether to adjust their trend-based projections for the coming year.

A less apparent impact between economic conditions and college and university revenues comes from the influence of the economy on enrollment levels. Analysts say the economy has "positive enrollment effects" when there is an increase in employment opportunities for college graduates or when the job market decreases for people who do not graduate from college (Paulsen, 1990). Depending on the type of institution, a strong economy either strengthens or weakens enrollment demand. Many two-year colleges, for instance, have found that their enrollments surge when jobs in the local community are scarce but dip when the economy rebounds. Community college administrators attribute this fluctuation to the need for the unemployed to be trained to reenter the workforce with new skills or expertise. Colleges with comparatively higher tuition charges, however, may have the opposite experience, as students become more price conscious during difficult economic periods.

Students and prospective students often think of attending college as a financial investment. Therefore, just as the economy affects other types of investments, it has an impact on college attendance as well. During the past decade, changes in the political economy have resulted in an increase in tuition and fees and a decrease in federal financial aid, which in turn affects enrollments. According to Paulsen (1990, p. 2.), "Student responsiveness to college cost decreases as income and academic ability rise, and vice versa."

Likewise, institutions in close proximity to large military facilities and government operations, such as capital cities, may also experience a fluctuation in enrollments based on the economy. When the economy is good, federal and state governments tend to be more willing to subsidize the cost of continuing education and training for their personnel. Colleges and universities in the Washington, D.C., area, for instance, report that the condition of the economy affects their enrollment in the classes that are used as training for government employees and paid for by the federal government.

Links Between Social Conditions and Revenue.   State and local appropriations for higher education depend not only on the strength of the area's economy but also on a variety of other factors that create competing priorities for governmental appropriations. Even with strong economies, many states have reduced appropriations to their colleges and universities in order to reallocate funds to other programs. During the past decade, higher education in most states has received a decreasing share of the state budget, as legislatures have responded to increased demands for law enforcement, corrections, health care, and welfare programs (see Figure 6.1).

Although the impact of external social conditions on state appropriations is mostly a concern for budget planners in public sector institutions, it also

Figure 6.1. Percentage of State Appropriation for Public Higher Education by Year, 1982–1994

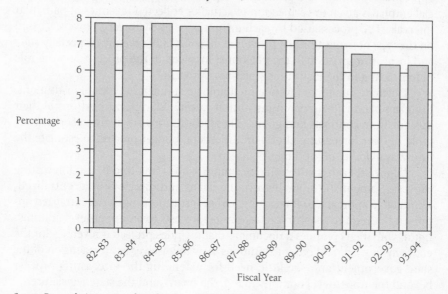

Source: Research Associates of Washington, 1994, p. 203. Used by permission.

should be of interest to many of their counterparts in the private sector, particularly in the twenty-two states assisting students to attend private colleges (DeSalvatore, 1996). In those states where students can receive state-funded tuition grants to attend the state's private colleges and universities, the amount of the grants is likely to be frozen or even reduced when the state needs to divert its resources to social programs.

A similar situation occurs at the federal level, where efforts to balance the budget and to absorb tax reductions are placing expenditure levels for existing programs under increased scrutiny. Planned spending reductions at the federal level for sponsored research or student financial aid can quickly translate into decreased revenue levels for institutions that are dependent on such programs.

Fundraising specialists are also encountering difficulty in obtaining support from the so-called yuppie generation. Many of today's donors, and especially those from the baby boom generation, seem to be more interested in supporting smaller units, such as a local nonprofit agency, rather than the larger, well-funded institutions (Strauss and Howe, 1991). This creates special challenges when forecasting revenue from private gifts.

Revenue Forecasting as a Process

(Material in the next two sections is based in part on telephone interviews with institutional officials around the country in midsummer of 1996.)

Forecasting revenues for institutions of higher education can be most appropriately viewed as a process. This process is typically ongoing, with special emphasis given to verification of actual or collected revenues at particular intervals. The process used by each institution is likely to vary, however, based on the type of institution, its predominant sources of revenue (especially state and local appropriations), the personnel involved in the process, and the role of forecasting in the institution's planning process.

Different sources of revenue predominate at different types of institutions. For example, major research institutions receive significant portions of their revenue from contracts and grants. These institutions are likely to concentrate more of their forecasting efforts on the federal budget process to estimate the future availability of funding.

Likewise, each institution determines who is involved in the forecasting process. Some institutions involve the deans and directors in a centralized, round table approach to forecasting. Other institutions use a decentralized approach but require each unit to report its forecasts to an upper-level administrator, who then compiles a document that includes projected revenues for the entire institution. Still other institutions view themselves as an extension of the state government and see little need for extending the forecasting process beyond the upper-level administrators, the board, and the state legislature.

Finally, institutions vary in the extent to which they incorporate revenue projections into their planning efforts. Linking revenue forecasts and institutional-planning exercises is important because the level of available revenue is likely to affect the development of new programs; the use of private contractors; the next tuition adjustment; and the repair, renovation, or construction of campus facilities.

Another important variable in the planning process is the time frame in which projections are made. Because many institutions are becoming more fiscally conservative, awareness of anticipated revenue prior to making budgetary commitments is critical. For example, different institutions create different parameters for fiscal planning. Public sector institutions are typically required to use an annual or biennial approach, whereas some private institutions prefer to plan using four- to five-year cycles. It is important for budget staff to determine a time line that is appropriate to the needs of their institution.

Most institutions that are on an annual fiscal time line begin to make revenue projections for the new fiscal year by December-January of the previous academic year. The forecasting process usually continues until the new fiscal year begins. Some institutions have a formal process with deadlines, formatting requirements, and presentations to governing boards and state legislatures. Other institutions rely on the chief financial officer or institutional researcher to do all the work and make most of the decisions.

The revenue-forecasting process also entails built-in, continuous monitoring of the actual revenue collected as well as the number of students who are actually attending versus the number who pre-enrolled. Typically, institutions conduct these interim reviews in October and February-March. Some, who have significant summer programs, may also monitor summer revenues and enrollments. These times of review are chosen in relation to the academic calendar and the drop-add process. Reviews range from monthly to as infrequently as annually. Institutions that are heavily funded by the state legislature may only review and update their revenue projections when the legislature reviews its budget, which is typically midterm of their annual budget cycle.

Many institutions must make adjustments to their projections and expenditure plans when a shortfall is discovered during the review of actual revenue. However, some have incorporated flexibility into their forecasts in order to create a reserve that enables them to allocate surplus revenue into deficit accounts when necessary.

The extent to which projections are reviewed also depends on the type of revenue that is being considered. For example, some institutions continuously review only those revenues that fund the Educational and General portions of their budgets; others limit their reviews to the revenue for auxiliary enterprises. The types of revenue over which the institution has the least amount of control tend to be the types that receive the most frequent attention (Meisinger, 1994).

Most institutions forecast revenues by incorporating one or more of the factors mentioned earlier in this chapter into a formula or model. However, institutions use a wide variety of models to incorporate these factors. Some institutions have staff who are able to develop sophisticated projection models that fit its particular needs. For example, Townsley (1994) provides a model used by Wilmington College, which incorporates short-term budget controls and benchmark equations to test actual budget performance against forecasts. The model was designed to address the particular needs of Wilmington as an "enrollment-dependent" college. Other institutions use models developed and published by national associations for business officers. Still others take existing models and adapt them to make the model more appropriate for use on their campuses. Models range from computer programs based on spreadsheet software, such as Lotus, to models that combine various methods and techniques. Gaylord (1983) categorizes approaches to forecasting revenues as judgmental (individual forecast, forecasting by committee-survey, and Delphi), time-series (trend curves, decomposition, exponential smoothing, Box-Jenkins or *ARIMA,* and *Bayesian*), and causal forecasting (single equation regression, simultaneous system, simulation, input-output, and cross-impact analysis).

Forecasting Techniques for Major Types of Revenue

As suggested above, the typical revenue-forecasting model is based on summing the independent projections for several different types of revenue—such as, student tuition and fees, governmental appropriations, governmental contracts and grants, private gifts, and auxiliary enterprises.

Each revenue stream depends on its own set of environmental factors. Various methods, both statistical and judgmental, are used to relate these factors to potential revenue. Each forecasting method is likely to include some type of historical assessment of revenue and expenditures, an estimate of future enrollment, and consideration of anticipated changes in the economic and social variables. The methods and factors most commonly used are described below for each of the revenue types.

Student Tuition and Fees. The effort to forecast tuition and fee revenues is a cyclical process at most institutions because decisions must be made annually on whether and how much to increase tuition and fees. These decisions are typically influenced by a variety of factors—high school graduation rates, market research, anticipated income from other revenue sources, anticipated expenditures, competitiveness of current tuition rates, enrollment projections, inflation rate, and tuition discounting provided by the institution.

When considering enrollment projections, budget staff must pay particular attention to specific student attributes, such as, part-time versus full-time, in-state versus out-of-state, and graduate versus undergraduate, which will affect the amount of revenue a student brings. Anticipated enrollment appears to be the most significant factor in the process. If students do not enroll and pay tuition and fees, the institution will be unable to function in its current mode.

Some public institutions, however, do not have the authority to set their own tuition schedules as they are required to operate within a statewide higher education–policy framework for tuition and other student charges. Likewise, "Public institutions typically are not free to retain revenues from increased tuition charges" (Becker, 1990, p. 162). Moreover, when forecasting the net contribution of tuition and fees, the institution's staff should consider including any information on discounts or scholarships that are provided by the institution itself or government funds that are earmarked for that purpose (Froomkin, 1990).

Governmental Appropriations. The need to develop a reliable capacity to project government appropriations is especially important for public sector institutions. The difficulty of this task for an institutional planner varies according to the way that the individual state develops its appropriations act.

In states where the executive budget office plays a strong role in the budget process, an institution is able to gain a reasonable estimate of its upcoming appropriation as soon as the governor's recommended budget is released. The projection can be especially accurate in those states where the appropriation for each institution is listed separately in the state budget.

The task is much more problematic, however, in states where the legislature is dominant in the budget development process. Institutional planners in those states not only have to take the governor's recommendation into account, but they also must monitor the progress of the appropriation bills in each of the legislative chambers. When the two bills vary considerably, the institution must await the report of the conference committee, often on the closing day of the session before it can begin planning for its own campus budget.

In some states, an institution may not be able to project its revenue from state appropriations even after the legislature adjourns. State higher education boards sometimes have responsibility for allocating the state appropriation among the public institutions. Institutions in these states must simulate formula-based allocation models to develop preliminary estimates of revenue from state appropriations.

Governmental Contracts and Grants. Interest in projecting revenue from contracts and grants varies considerably from one institution to another. This revenue source is not much of an issue for some institutions, such as community colleges and liberal arts institutions that are focused on teaching and that attract relatively few federal dollars for sponsored research. Their primary focus in monitoring the federal budget development process is on the amounts to be appropriated for student financial aid programs.

The situation is much different, of course, for major research universities that rely heavily on sponsored-program revenue for their operations. In some ways, the task of projecting sponsored revenue is perhaps less challenging than for other sources, but in other ways it is much more difficult. In many cases, an institution's revenues from federal sources are through multiyear grants and contracts. For these funds, the revenue planner needs only to review individual grant documents to determine how much will be released during the coming year.

The special challenges in projecting contract and grant revenue come from the fact that competition for these funds is quite strong, and federal priorities can shift rapidly depending on changes in administrations, Congress, economic conditions, and international tensions. Unlike state appropriations where many public officials are concerned about ensuring some degree of stability in the appropriations process for each agency, contracts and grants are often awarded competitively. It is not uncommon for contract and grant revenues to fluctuate by 10 percent or more from one year to the next, depending on the success of individual researchers in attracting federal awards.

A second challenge in projecting contract and grant revenue is that the amounts appropriated to various federal programs can vary considerably over time. As amounts appropriated for the national defense have slipped in recent years, so have the amounts available for defense-related research. Although some institutions have strength in sufficiently diverse areas of research to absorb shifting patterns of federal investment from one focus to another, such as from defense to health care, other institutions are much more vulnerable to changing federal priorities.

Private Gifts. The approach toward projecting revenues from private giving-endowments most often depends on the individual institution. Some institutions have large endowments and must keep a close watch on the economy in an effort to anticipate changes in interest rates and the trends in private giving. It is also important for the staff of institutions to carefully examine and document the institution's own trends in private giving and investments.

Some institutions, particularly most community colleges, have little or no endowment or private giving. Therefore, little or no forecasting is necessary for this type of revenue at these colleges. However, with the decline in federal and state support of higher education, it is likely that most, if not all, institutions will soon find it necessary to focus more on raising private funds, which in turn will increase the importance of valid revenue projection models for private giving.

In several cases, institutions or governing boards may determine specific institutional needs that depend on fundraising efforts. These needs are often established as revenue goals for which institutional fundraisers must aim. Recently, more institutions are establishing planned-giving campaigns in an effort to gain long-term commitment from donors. This should make projecting this type of revenue more predictable.

Auxiliary Enterprises.   It is managers of the auxiliary enterprises programs, rather than central budget planners, who typically do forecasting for their own revenues. They also determine new product lines or services and associated charges. For example, the addition of T-shirts to the campus bookstore is generally a decision of the bookstore manager, as is the price of such items; campus budget staff and budget committees need not be involved. On the other hand, some product-service-pricing decisions in auxiliaries—for example, housing rates—are likely to require consultation with, and even approval from, other offices on campus or the central budget process.

Another example is when the campus food service is operated as an auxiliary. If the food service management determines the need to increase the price of the meal plans they offer, typically steps must be taken to gain approval from either the institution's administration or from a committee designed to oversee the food service operation, or approval from both. This committee traditionally consists of faculty, staff, and students. The reason this type of revenue increase must undergo such scrutiny is because it more directly affects student costs than does the addition of a new product line in the bookstore. Also, students will have a choice whether or not to purchase a T-shirt in the bookstore, but they may find it necessary to eat in the campus cafeteria.

This process will depend on the institution's policy in regard to auxiliary enterprises or on the contract the auxiliary has with an external vendor through privatization. Therefore, each institution may handle it differently.

After the auxiliary managers make their own revenue projections, their forecasts are typically shared with the institution's budget officer as part of the effort to determine the overall institutional revenue for the upcoming year.

Summary and Conclusions

Revenue forecasting is the critical first step in most institutions' budget-planning processes. Though it seems a straightforward exercise, effective revenue forecasting requires consideration of the interaction among a number of variables in an institution's internal and external environments, including demographic trends, economic conditions, and broad social priorities. The challenge facing institutional budget planners is in determining which environmental variables have the most impact on future revenues for their institutions.

References

Becker, W. E. "The Demand for Higher Education." In S. A. Hoenack and E. L. Collins (eds.), *The Economics of Higher Education: Management, Operations, and Fiscal Environment.* Albany: State University of New York Press, 1990.

Brinkman, P. T. "College and University Adjustments to a Changing Financial Environment." In S. A. Hoenack and E. L. Collins (eds.), *The Economics of Higher Education: Management, Operations, and Fiscal Environment.* Albany: State University of New York Press, 1990.

DeSalvatore, K. *The National Association of State Student Grant & Aid Programs Annual Report for the 1994–95 Academic Year.* New York: New York State Higher Education Services Corporation, 1996.

Froomkin, J. "The Impact of Changing Levels of Financial Resources on the Structure of Colleges and Universities." In S. A. Hoenack and E. L. Collins (eds.), *The Economics of Higher Education: Management, Operations, and Fiscal Environment.* Albany: State University of New York Press, 1990.

Gaylord, T. "An Approach to Quantitative Fiscal Planning: Phase 1 Report." Alaska State Department of Education, Statewide Office of Budget Development, 1983. (ED 239 551)

Meisinger, R. J. *College and University Budgeting: An Introduction for Faculty and Academic Administrators.* (2nd ed.) Washington, D.C.: National Association of College and University Business Officers, 1994.

Paulsen, M. B. "College Choice: Understanding Student Enrollment Behavior." ASHE-ERIC Higher Education Report, no. 6. Washington, D.C.: School of Education and Human Development, George Washington University, 1990. (ED 333 855)

Research Associates of Washington. *State Profiles: Financing Public Higher Education 1978–1994.* (17th ed.) Washington, D.C.: Research Associates of Washington, 1994.

Ryan, E. "New Approaches to the Well." *Currents,* 1994, *20* (2), 40–45.

Strauss, W., and Howe, N. *Generations: The History of America's Future, 1584 to 2069.* New York: Morrow, 1991.

Townsley, M. K. "Deficit Prevention: Budget Control Model for Enrollment-Dependent Colleges." *NACUBO Business Officer,* 1994, *28* (4), 40–44.

U.S. Department of Education, National Center for Education Statistics, Integrated Postsecondary Education Data System. *Finance Survey.* Washington, D.C.: U.S. Government Printing Office, 1995.

J. KENT CARUTHERS *is senior partner with MGT of America, Inc., a higher education consulting firm. He is a part-time faculty member at the College of Education, Florida State University (Tallahassee).*

CATHI L. WENTWORTH *is a doctoral degree candidate in the higher education administration program at the College of Education, Florida State University.*

There are several important lessons to be learned about enrollment and revenue forecasting in the previous chapters.

The Future Is Now: Limitations of the Crystal Ball and Other Lessons Learned

Daniel T. Layzell

Institutional researchers are often forced into the role of oracle in divining the answers to various policy questions. This is especially true in the areas of enrollment and revenue forecasting. The chapters in this volume have explored a variety of facets to these critical activities, ranging from the demographic and economic trends facing higher education to the methods and techniques used in enrollment and revenue forecasting and to the experiences of public and private institutions in effecting these types of forecasts. They also present a set of useful lessons and limitations to be heeded by institutional researchers and others as they attempt to divine the future. This chapter outlines the major lessons presented in the previous chapters and makes some suggestions for the practice of institutional research. It also presents some supplemental resources for institutional researchers to use in these important activities.

Lessons Learned

The six major lessons learned in the previous chapters are described in the next several sections.

Lesson One: Higher Education's Environment Is Changing. As indicated at the beginning of this volume, higher education is in an era of change. The chapters by Zúñiga and Hauptman indicate well the changing demographic and economic conditions in which higher education operates. The size of the pool of traditional college-age students is definitely expected to grow over the next several years, and the number of nontraditional students is expected to at least remain stable. However, as Zúñiga notes, demography is not destiny in predicting how these trends will affect future enrollments. On the financial side of the house, public and private institutions of higher education are becoming more tuition dependent, especially as state funding for higher education continues to stagnate. This is significant because the latitude that an institution has in raising tuition rates is constrained by the effects of price-elasticity on enrollment (for example, the extent to which enrollments are affected by changes in tuition). Institutions with relatively inelastic demand will have more latitude in raising prices than those whose traditional clientele are price sensitive (for example, community colleges).

Further, the delivery of higher education is changing through the advent of distance education and other instructional technologies. Also, there is a continued movement toward lifelong learning because the changing economy is forcing adults to constantly retool their skills and knowledge to remain competitive in the job market. All of these factors will affect enrollment- and revenue-forecasting efforts in the future.

Lesson Two: There Are Significant Differences Among the Sectors of Higher Education.   Hauptman's chapter makes an important point that is sometimes forgotten—all institutions are *not* created equal, and therefore the policy issues they face are often different. This reinforces the point that there is no single forecasting method or technique that works for all institutions—be it in enrollment or revenue forecasting. For example, on the funding side, a community college may well be concerned about local support for an increase in the property tax levy, whereas a major research university is going to be concerned about what is going on in Washington in the congressional committees that appropriate funds for federally sponsored research projects. As noted by Caruthers and Wentworth, "The challenge facing institutional budget planners is in determining which environmental variables have the most impact on future revenues for their institutions." The same principle is true when discussing the issue of enrollment when it is clear that different institutions serve different types of students.

The chapter by Peters and Keihn and the chapter by Day provide useful illustrations of the different sets of issues faced by a large public university system and by private institutions. In Wisconsin, the issue of enrollment planning for the University of Wisconsin System has been a highly politicized activity in a state that has traditionally prided itself on providing a high level of access to public higher education to its citizens but now finds itself dealing with the same budget constraints faced by countless other states. On the other hand, enrollment and revenue planning in private institutions is largely a market-driven enterprise and is addressed in much the same way as a company plans for new and existing product lines.

Lesson Three: Enrollment and Revenue Forecasting Is Both Art and Science.   The chapter by Brinkman and McIntyre and the chapter by Caruthers and Wentworth illustrate the technical boundaries of enrollment- and revenue-forecasting methodologies. The methods and techniques used in forecasting have without a doubt been improved and refined over the past several years—largely due to technological advancements. However, given that the r-square is never 1.000 no matter how sophisticated the forecasting model, there is always going to be an element of forecasting enrollment and revenue that draws on the innate judgment and experience of the analyst—the "gut instinct" factor.

Lesson Four: Some Factors Are Controllable; Others Are Not. Closely related to the previously mentioned lesson is the fact that, when engaging in forecasting exercises, analysts should keep in mind those factors that are outside the control of the institution. For example, as noted by Caruthers and Wentworth, the ability of public institutions to forecast a major source of operating revenue—state appropriations—is largely subject to legislative behavior, which is difficult to predict for those outside the political process (and sometimes for those inside!). Although tuition charges and admissions criteria are often in the control of the institution, general social, political, demographic, and economic forces are not.

However, neither can the analyst afford to ignore these trends. As noted by Brinkman and McIntyre, "These unmanageable factors are at work, and ignoring them may well result in inaccurate forecasts. Even though one has little if any control over them, it is imperative that their impact on enrollment be assessed so that actions that can be managed are more likely to have the intended results." Likewise, Caruthers and Wentworth posit that "effective revenue forecasting requires consideration of the interaction among a number of variables in an institution's internal and external environments." In short, do not bet the house on factors outside the institution's control, but do not forget them either.

Lesson Five: Higher Education Is Increasingly Operating in a Competitive and Open Marketplace. The decline in the public subsidy for higher education has certainly forced colleges and universities into a more competitive posture with regard to the provision of educational services. In addition, the higher education marketplace itself is changing. The identification of niche markets and the demand for specialized programs are shaping the way higher education institutions are beginning to think about their businesses. As indicated in a recent Pew Trust publication, "Emerging in its stead is a commodity market in which an increasing proportion of students are buying their education 'one course at a time' from a variety of vendors which these students consider principally as outlets for educational services" (Pew Charitable Trusts, 1996, p. 3). In sum, the delivery of higher education services is becoming much more consumer driven than at any time in recent history.

At the same time, degree-granting proprietary institutions are moving into competition with traditional colleges and universities for both traditional-age students and working adults. As indicated by Day, private institutions have always been market driven in their forecasting efforts; public institutions must now join the fray. Together, these changes suggest a need for increasingly sophisticated methodologies that take into account the behavior of both students and competitors.

Lesson Six: Forecasting Methods and Techniques Are Only a Tool to Aid Good Management, Not a Substitute. A common theme throughout all of the chapters is the need to balance data analysis with good judgment and process in applying forecasting methods and techniques. For those institutions that have solid, flexible, and resilient management structures in place, the application of the methods outlined in the previous chapters can help further the operation of the institution. However, technology can never be a substitute for good management, no matter how sophisticated the method or technique.

Additional Resources

Each of the preceding chapters lists a number of excellent sources of literature in its bibliography, which are commended to the reader for further exploration. The following are a few selections readers may especially want to pursue:

Anderson, R. E., and Meyerson, J. W. (eds.). *Financial Planning Under Economic Uncertainty.* New Directions for Higher Education, no. 69. San Francisco: Jossey-Bass, 1990.

Callan, P. M. (ed.). *Environmental Scanning for Strategic Leadership.* New Directions for Institutional Research, no. 52. San Francisco: Jossey-Bass, 1986.

Hossler, D., Bean, J. P., and Associates. *The Strategic Management of College Enrollments.* San Francisco: Jossey-Bass, 1990.

Jordan, S. M. "Enrollment Demand in Arizona: Policy Choices and Social Consequences." In J. I. Gill and L. Saunders (eds.), *Developing Effective Policy Analysis in Higher Education.* New Directions for Institutional Research, no. 76. San Francisco: Jossey-Bass, 1992.

Morrison, J. L., and Mecca, T. V. "Managing Uncertainty: Environmental Analysis/Forecasting in Academic Planning." In J. C. Smart (ed.), *Higher Education: Handbook of Theory and Research,* vol. 5. New York: Agathon Press, 1989.

Wing, P. *Higher Education Enrollment Forecasting: A Manual for State-Level Agencies.* Boulder, Colo.: National Center for Higher Education Management Systems, 1974.

In addition, the following publications and organizations have World Wide Web sites providing access to or descriptions of useful articles, research reports, and data related to enrollment and financial issues:

American Demographics (a magazine that includes articles on demographic trends and issues). [http://www.demographics.com].

American Association of State Colleges and Universities. [http://www.ags.com/market/AASCU/aascu.htm].

Association for Institutional Research. [http://www.fsu.edu/~air/home.htm].

The College Board. [http://www.collegeboard.org].

Higher Education Research Institute, University of California-Los Angeles. [http://www.gseis.ucla.edu/heri/heri.html].

National Center for Education Statistics. [http://www.ed.gov/NCES].

On the Horizon (an environmental-scanning newsletter for education professionals). [http://sunsite.unc.edu/horizon].

U.S. Bureau of the Census. [http://www.census.gov].

Reference

Pew Charitable Trusts (Philadelphia). "Rumbling." *Policy Perspectives*, 1996, 7 (1).

DANIEL T. LAYZELL is senior associate with MGT of America, Inc., a higher education consulting firm in Tallahassee, Florida. He was previously (until March 1997) director of policy analysis and research for the University of Wisconsin System.

INDEX

ORDERING INFORMATION

NEW DIRECTIONS FOR INSTITUTIONAL RESEARCH is a series of paperback books that provides planners and administrators in all types of academic institutions with guidelines in such areas as resource coordination, information analysis, program evaluation, and institutional management. Books in the series are published quarterly in spring, summer, fall, and winter and are available for purchase by subscription as well as by single copy.

SUBSCRIPTIONS cost $52.00 for individuals (a savings of 35 percent over single-copy prices) and $79.00 for institutions, agencies, and libraries. Please do not send institutional checks for personal subscriptions. Standing orders are accepted.

SINGLE COPIES cost $20.00 plus shipping (see below) when payment accompanies order. California, New Jersey, New York, and Washington, D.C., residents please include appropriate sales tax. Canadian residents add GST and any local taxes. Billed orders will be charged shipping and handling. No billed shipments to post office boxes. Orders from outside the United States or Canada *must be prepaid* in U.S. dollars or charged to VISA, MasterCard, or American Express.

SHIPPING (SINGLE COPIES ONLY): $10.00 and under, add $2.50; $10.01–$20, add $3.50; $20.01–$50, add $4.50; $50.01–$75, add $5.50; $75.01–$100, add $6.50; $100.01–$150, add $7.50; over $150, add $8.50. Outside of North America, please add $15.00 per book for priority shipment.

DISCOUNTS FOR QUANTITY ORDERS are available. Please write to the address below for information.

ALL ORDERS must include either the name of an individual or an official purchase order number. Please submit your order as follows:
   Subscriptions: specify series and year subscription is to begin
   Single copies: include individual title code (such as IR78)

MAIL ALL ORDERS TO:
   Jossey-Bass Publishers
   350 Sansome Street
   San Francisco, CA 94104-1342

FOR SUBSCRIPTION SALES OUTSIDE OF THE UNITED STATES, CONTACT:
any international subscription agency or Jossey-Bass directly.

OTHER TITLES AVAILABLE IN THE
NEW DIRECTIONS FOR INSTITUTIONAL RESEARCH SERIES
J. Fredericks Volkwein, Editor-in-Chief